THE
COMPLETE
SERGER
HANDBOOK

THE COMPLETE SERGER HANDBOOK

Chris James

Sterling Publishing Co., Inc.,
New York

A Sterling/Sewing Information Resources Book

Sewing Information Resources

Owner: JoAnn Pugh-Gannon
Photography: Kaz Ayukawa, K Graphics
Book Design and Electronic Page Layout: Ernie Shelton, Shelton Design Studios, Inc.

Library of Congress Cataloging-in-Publication Data Available.

James, Chris.
    The complete serger handbook / Chris James.
    p.   cm.
    "A Sterling/Sewing Information Resources book".
    Includes index.
    ISBN 0-8069-9806-7
    1. Serging. 2. Sewing machines. I. Title.
TT713.J36   1997
646.2'044—dc21   96-39316
                                        CIP

A Sterling/Sewing Information Resources Book

2 4 6 8 10 9 7 5 3 1

Distributed by Sterling Publishing Company, Inc.
387 Park Avenue South, New York, N.Y. 10016
Published by Sewing Information Resources
P.O. Box 330, Wasco, Il. 60183
©1997 by Chris James
Distributed in Canada by Sterling Publishing
c/o Canadian Manda Group, One Atlantic Avenue, Suite 105
Toronto, Ontario, Canada, N6K 3E7
Distributed in Great Britain and Europe by Cassell PLC
Wellington House, 125 Strand, London WC2R 0BB, England
Distributed in Australia by Capricorn Link (Australia) Pty Ltd.
P.O. Box 6651, Baulkham Hills, Business Centre, NSW 2153, Australia
Printed in Hong Kong
All rights reserved.

Sterling ISBN 0-8069-9806-7

Chris James has taught sewing to others who share her passion for fabric and thread for over twenty years. Her first love is using the overlock machine or serger, concentrating on investigating and teaching serging techniques for the past fourteen years. In classes from 3 to 98, she shares her students successes while happily continuing to learn from them, also. In fact, she is often invited to go home with her students just to be there to answer their serger questions! Challenging international teaching assignments include teaching non-English speaking Japanese men and women how to make a buttonhole and thread a serger.

As a Sewing Specialist for Bernina of America for nine years, Chris traveled extensively sharing her knowledge and herself with other sewing enthusiasts. She wrote educational and training materials for the Bernina dealers and authored a home decorating booklet, A Collection of Cushions to Sew Yourself, which concentrated on serging techniques. Her work has appeared in Butterick and Vogue magazines and pattern books, numerous sewing and quilting magazines and the Bernina Creative Sewing magazine. She has also consulted on numerous craft and garment patterns.

DEDICATION

To GeeGee

Thanks to my boys, Brian and Jon, for trying to understand, "I can't, I'm working on the book"; JoAnn Pugh-Gannon for her faith, confidence and patience, her friendship and guidance and for all her time spent making me look good; David Gunzburger for the encouragement and perspective; and lastly, all of my students over the years who asked me to do this, and kept asking...

TABLE OF CONTENTS

Introduction

Prologue — Can Your Serger Replace Your Sewing Machine? — 10

Chapter 1 — Getting to Know Your Machine — 12

Definition — 14
Identifying Serger Parts — 15
Needles — 23
Serger Tools - Traditional and Some Surprises — 25

Chapter 2 — Threads, Threads, and More Threads! — 28

Threads — 30
Thread Quality or There's No Such Thing as a Bargain — 30
Thread Packaging — 30
Thread Weight - Unraveling the Code — 33
Thread Type - Polyester, Cotton or What??? — 34
Should All Serger Threads Match? — 40

Chapter 3 — Which Stitch is Which?? — 42

Focus on Basic Serger Stitch Formations — 44
2-Thread Overlock Stitch — 45
2-Thread Chainstitch — 45
3-Thread Overlock Stitch — 46
4-Thread Overlock Stitch — 47
4-Thread Safety Stitch — 48
5-Thread Safety Stitch — 48
Cover Stitch or Cover Hem — 49

Chapter 4 — Threading and Rethreading — 50

Take the Terror Out of Troubleshooting! — 60
Threading Shortcuts or the "Really Easy"
Way to Thread a Serger — 62

Chapter 5 — Take the Tension Out of Tension Theory — 64

Tension: A Definition — 66
Tension Knobs, Dials, and Slides — 66
The Perfect Overlock Stitch — 68
The Not-So-Perfect Overlock Stitch — 71
TNT — 71
Thread Type — 72
Fabric Weight — 73
Stitch Length — 74
Stitch Width — 74
Tension Disk Cleaning and Maintenance — 76
Some Odds and Ends on Tension Management — 77

Chapter 6 — Investigating Serger Controls — 78

Stitch Length — 80
Cutting Width — 82
Differential Feed — 83
Presser Foot Pressure Control — 86

Chapter 7 — Mastering Serger Techniques — 88

The Presser Foot — 90
Serger Seams - Guiding the Fabric — 91
Serger Seams - Securing the Seam — 94

Removing Serger Seams _____ 97
Serging Corners _____ 99
Serging Curves _____ 103
Serging in a Circle _____ 104
Using the Serger to Hem _____ 105

Chapter 8   Unraveling Knit Nonsense _____ 106

The Many Faces of Knit Fabrics _____ 108
Setting Up the Overlock Machine for the Best Results _____ 109
Construction _____ 111
    Taping Seams _____ 112
    Ribbing _____ 113
    Hemming Knit Fabrics _____ 115
    A Primer on Elastic _____ 116
    Applications - Casings or Direct? _____ 118
Lycra _____ 119
Tricot _____ 121

Chapter 9   Rolled Hem Riot _____ 122

The Needle _____ 124
Stitch Width _____ 124
Stitch Length _____ 125
Rolled Hem Tension Settings _____ 126
Notes on Fabric and Threads _____ 127
Rolled Hem Challenges _____ 129
Uses for the Rolled Hem _____ 132

Chapter 10   Flatlocking - Functional and Fun _____ 134

Flatlocking - Let's Get Technical _____ 136
    2-Thread Flatlock _____ 137
    3-Thread Flatlock _____ 137
    3-Thread Flatlock with Three Visible Threads _____ 139
    4-Thread or Safety Stitch Flatlock _____ 139
    Needles and Fabric _____ 140
    Thread _____ 140
    Stitch Width _____ 141
    Stitch Length _____ 141
    Cutting Width _____ 141
It's Time to Serge, but Some Reminders First _____ 142
Troubleshooting a Flatlock Stitch _____ 143
If It Looks like a Flatlock, Is It Always a Flatlock? _____ 144
False Flatlock Stitches _____ 146
Using the Flatlock Stitch _____ 148
    Hems _____ 148
    Flatlocking Elastic _____ 149
    Flatlocking Fake Fur or Heavily Textured Fabric _____ 149
    Flatlock Fringe _____ 150
    Flatlock Thread Casings _____ 150
    Flatlocking with Lace _____ 151
    A Final Word on Flatlocking _____ 151

Appendix A   Oh No! My Serger is Sick! _____ 152

Appendix B   The Care and Feeding of Your Overlock Machine _____ 155

Index _____ 156

purchased and used my first serger in 1979. (It is important that I bought and used it in the same time frame, but more about that later.) I have to admit that my purchase was motivated by a bit of laziness and lots of financial need. I was sewing for a children's boutique in Washington, D.C., making corduroy and denim overalls and jumpers and little girls' dresses and pinafores. My instruc-

tions were to construct using French seams on lightweight fabrics and flat fell seams on the heavier fabrics. Honestly, I was being paid piecework and it was not enough for the time it would take me to do these specialized techniques. There had to be a way to speed up my sewing, but maintain the quality of my work. Thus, a serger!

My first serger was not what you would call "user friendly." It had no light, no numbers on the tension dials, the tension dials went around 19 times, and I don't think I ever figured out how to adjust the stitch length. I used it to finish seams only, using the settings as they were when the machine came out of the box. Fortunately, that has all changed. Machines are easier to thread, use, adjust, and maintain. They have become the microwave or CD player of the sewing world. You really don't know if you need one, but once you have it you don't know how you ever lived without it.

Over the past 15 years, I have taught thousands of students, in classes of 3 to 98 people, to use and enjoy their serger. Many times I heard comments such as, "I have had my serger for 3 months (or 6 months, or a year), but this is the first time

I've had it out of the box." My other favorite is, "My husband (or mother, sister) bought this for me and I don't have a clue what it does." At the end of class, these same students were tired, enlightened, and excited about this wonderful new machine they owned. They have offered me lavish accommodations if I would come home with them and be there when they want to serge. Even though they took notes they wanted a handout of everything I had said. I wish I could have taken them up on some of the invitations home, but instead here's the complete handout. Use it, digest the information, and then read it again.

This book is for the novice first taking the serger out of the box to the experienced serger user who needs a reminder about a certain technique not used in quite some time. It is meant to be a reference, an additional instruction book, a serging friend, and hidden between the lines, an inspiration. Place it next to your machine and refer to it often. A serger is fast, fun, and offers many opportunities for creativity, once it has been taken out of the box!

Give yourself time to develop a "serger mode," a time to recognize where a serger stitch will replace a sewing machine technique, whether it be for finishing edges, garment construction or decorative work. It will take time to learn to use your serger efficiently on your projects; you were not an instant sewing machine expert, but soon you may find yourself earning a nickname given me by my favorite 12-year-old student – "The Serger Maniac." Good Luck and Enjoy!

Question: Can an overlock machine replace a sewing machine?

Answer: No, Yes, Sometimes, Sort of, Depends

You have heard about, asked about, talked about, and maybe even used a serger. You are still not sure if you want (or need?) one because you already have a perfectly good sewing machine that you dearly love. (The question of need is another whole book. Consider the snow blower or a garden tiller that is used once a year vs. a machine that will be used regularly. Also don't forget the most important thing, you deserve it!) So, to justify it you ask: Can an overlock machine replace a sewing machine? The answer seems to be double talk, but it really is not. The answer is, no it cannot, yes it can, sometimes it will, it sort of does, and depends!!

Read on for the explanation.

NO, IT CANNOT - There are situations when the serger cannot replace a sewing machine, not many, but still important ones. The simple reply once was, sergers cannot replace sewing machines. You cannot insert zippers or make buttonholes. Well sergers do insert beautiful zippers, but buttonholes in the traditional sense are out. Some books offer buttonhole directions, but it's stretching it a bit. A serger also cannot accurately serge around tight curves or sharp angles. The presser foot is too big and visibility less than is needed. If serging must start and stop at a specific point and absolute accuracy is essential, the sewing machine is the better tool. Finally, if fit is in question, it is not wise to use a machine that cuts off the extra fabric!

YES, IT CAN - The overlock machine can replace the sewing machine for many procedures that are less than exciting. Long straight seams are much faster and finished when using the serger. In many cases, a multiple step process done on

the sewing machine can be changed into one step on the overlock. Fabrics that may have been avoided on the sewing machine because they stretch, pill or ravel, or are hard to control and guide are sewn nearly effortlessly on the overlock. It may take time to replace the sewing machine as much as is possible because you need experience to see where using a serger is possible, but, the more you serge, the more you will serge.

SOMETIMES AND SORT OF - Somewhere there are directions for doing just about anything on the serger. This includes everything from button-holes, to making lace, to quilting, to appliqué. These techniques are explained and done in a "serger mode," so serger lace looks very different from traditional lace and appliqué means serging around something and then sewing it to something else with a sewing machine. The serger is used, but not always in the way one may expect. Sometimes the overlock way may be preferred, sometimes another way is better.

DEPENDS - The amount of time that an overlock machine will replace the sewing machine depends on the individual using it. It will depend on which is more important, speed and a slightly rounded corner, or a bit more time spent

and a perfect 90° corner. Is the baby dress being constructed on the sewing machine to become a family heirloom with detail upon detail absolutely flawless, or one done quickly on the serger that will be worn and washed many, many times? Is the quilt to be a cherished treasure, or one the dog will share with a child? Are there hours available to create and enjoy the process or valued minutes when the project must be done? The serger user will have to decide, but the discovery will surely be made that, the more the serger is used, the more it will be used.

CONSTRUCTION

Note: All seam allowances are 5/8" wide.

FABRIC KEY

RIGHT SIDE

WRONG SIDE

GETTING TO KNOW YOUR MACHINE

Sergers come in many shapes, colors, sizes, and degrees of sophistication. Some have knobs, some slide switches. Some have an LED screen, some have stitch selection dials that set the tension, and some have no references at all! Every serger, even those of the same make and model, operate and feel a bit different. Just like the first time you drive a new car, you must learn the location and operation of all the controls. This chapter is the study guide for your "Serger Driver's Test."

Definition

Let's first identify and define the machine you are using. In today's sewing world, the name serger and overlock are used synonymously to mean a compact machine that quickly trims, seams, and overcasts the edge of a piece of fabric in one operation. To be technical, the name of the stitch formed is industry recognized as an overlock stitch, thus the machine is an overlock machine or overlocker. The act of using the machine is serging, thus a serger. Both names are recognized, used in print instruction and information, and considered correct.

The commercial market has used the serger or overlock machine in factories since the early 1900's. The factory machines are large, heavy, and loud. Their motors are usually separate, not enclosed in the housing of the machine. They serge almost three times as fast as the domestic models and the older machines may have few safety features. Often they are designed to do one specific task and operators do not select stitch types or settings. Their cost may be three to five times that of a domestic machine. They serge well and for long hours, but they are not practical for personal use.

In 1967, the first personal-use serger was introduced. Double knit garments were in their heyday in ready-to-wear. This compact machine, that did a stitch "just like ready-to-wear," was perfect. It quickly found a secure place in the hearts and homes of all sewers. Over the years, we have discovered that sergers are not just for sewing knits, they are for virtually all fabrics, and new techniques or variations on old techniques are discovered daily.

Identifying Serger Parts

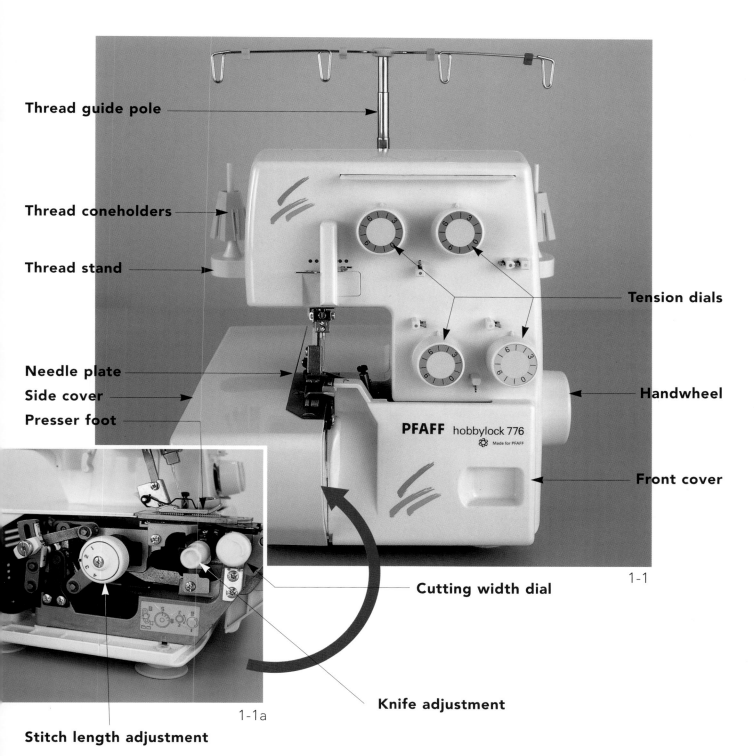

Thread guide pole

Thread coneholders

Thread stand

Needle plate

Side cover

Presser foot

Tension dials

Handwheel

PFAFF hobbylock 776
Made for PFAFF

Front cover

1-1

Cutting width dial

Stitch length adjustment

1-1a

Knife adjustment

Identifying Serger Parts

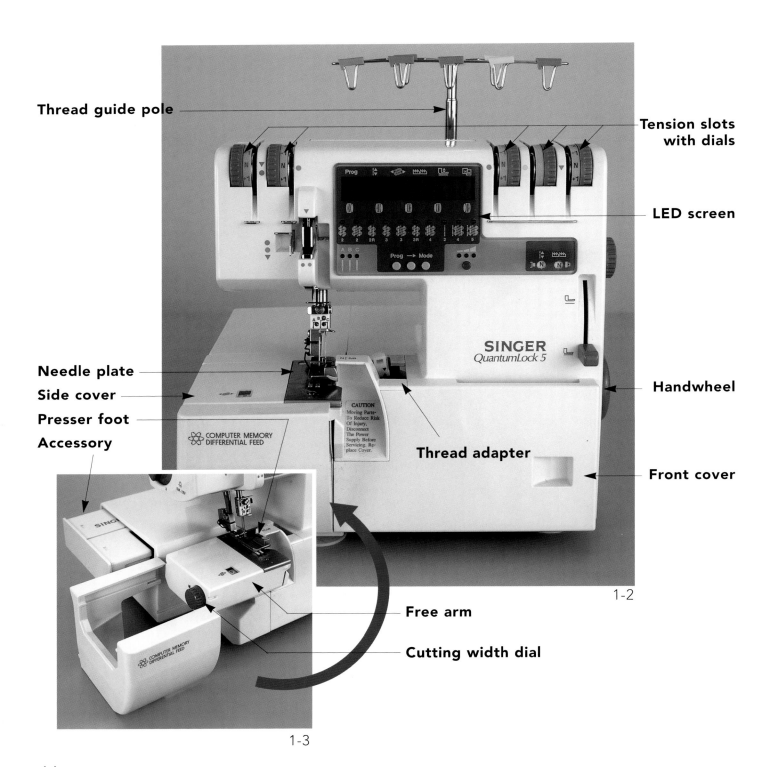

Thread guide pole

Tension slots with dials

LED screen

Needle plate

Side cover

Presser foot

Accessory

SINGER
QuantumLock 5

CAUTION
Moving Parts-
To Reduce Risk
Of Injury,
Disconnect
The Power
Supply Before
Servicing. Re-
place Cover.

Thread adapter

Handwheel

Front cover

COMPUTER MEMORY
DIFFERENTIAL FEED

1-2

Free arm

Cutting width dial

1-3

Identifying Serger Parts

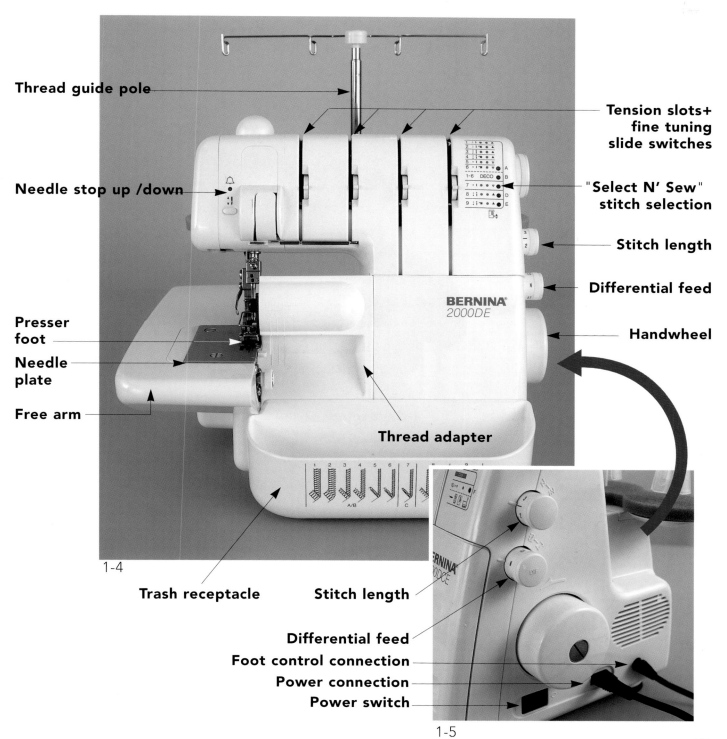

Thread guide pole

Needle stop up /down

Presser foot

Needle plate

Free arm

1-4

Tension slots+ fine tuning slide switches

"Select N' Sew" stitch selection

Stitch length

Differential feed

Handwheel

BERNINA
2000DE

Thread adapter

Trash receptacle

Stitch length

Differential feed

Foot control connection

Power connection

Power switch

1-5

GETTING
TO KNOW
YOUR
MACHINE

The location of key parts and controls on different brands and models, and even models within the same brand, may slightly differ. Compare the machines shown here to the picture or diagram found in your instruction manual. You may want to photocopy the one in your manual and keep it near your machine for easy reference.

Power Switch - The power switch is usually found on the right side of the machine. Some models have two "on" positions, one turning on the power and light, the second position, just power. Older models do not have a power switch, but are always "on" when the machine is plugged in. Be sure to unplug this model machine when it is not in use.

Light Switch - Some machines have a light switch separate from the power switch. Many people leave the light switch "on" all the time as a visual indicator that the machine is on or off. Before replacing what seems to be a burnt out light bulb, check this switch to make sure it is in the "on" position.

1-6

◄ **Handwheel** - The handwheel on the serger is located on the right side of the machine. On most recent models, the handwheel turns toward you, or counterclockwise just like a sewing machine. The handwheel on older models may turn clockwise or away from you. Most likely, there is an arrow on the machine or handwheel indicating the correct direction. Rotating the handwheel the wrong way can tangle and break threads resulting in rethreading and cause mechanical problems.

Foot Control and Foot Control ▶ Socket - The serger foot control plugs into a socket located near the power switch. It can have a separate cord or be part of the machine power cord. Originally, serging speed could be controlled with foot pressure. Now, foot controls may have switches with 2- or 3-speed settings. The newest feature is a "cruise control" type setting. Without increased pressure on the foot control, the machine maintains

1-7

the same needle penetration power and speeds through heavy or thick fabrics or multi-layer intersections as easily as it serges through lightweight ones.

One brand of serger controls the serging speed with a small slide switch located on the front of the machine rather than with pressure exerted on the foot control. Using the recognized symbols of speed, the tortoise and the hare, this switch can be set anywhere between maximum (the hare) and minimum (the tortoise). ▶

1-8

Thread Stand and Guide Pole - The thread guide pole must be extended to its highest position and facing in the correct direction for consistent, good stitch quality. An arrow on top of the pole indicates which direction is "forward." The thread stand or spool base supports the spool pins on which the thread is placed. Some thread stands have sponge pieces, felt circles, or plastic disks at the base of the spool pins to quiet the rattling of the thread cones and help the thread feed smoothly. Coneholders placed on spool pins will also help to stabilize the cone thread, especially when serging at high speed.

Front Cover or Looper Cover - The front cover prevents lint, fabric, dust, and your fingers from coming into contact with moving parts. Safety considerations make it necessary to slide or raise the cover to open. Some machines have a button or lever to release the cover door. When opened, this cover reveals the loopers and thread guides and usually a convenient threading diagram. Accessories may also be stored on this cover. For safety reasons, some machines will not operate with this door open.

Loopers - The loopers carry the threads that interlock with the needle threads to form the serger stitch. When forming a 3- or 4-thread balanced overlock stitch, the upper looper thread sits on top of the fabric, the lower looper thread on the under side. The eye of the loopers is large so it can carry heavier, thicker threads that can't pass through the needle eye. Depending on the machine and stitch formation selected, all or just one looper may be used.

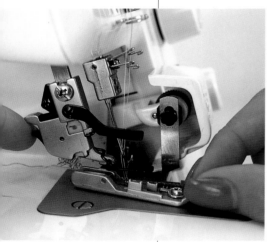

1-9

Side Cover - This cover swings to the left to open and has a lever or button as its release mechanism. It keeps lint, fabric, and fingers from moving parts and may also automatically cut off power when opened. When threading, an open side cover offers more light and open space for visibility. Machines with a free arm will not have a side cover.

◄ **Presser Foot and Presser Foot Lifter** - The presser foot holds the fabric against the feed dogs. Most newer-model machines have snap-on feet. This makes them easy to remove and allows greater visibility when threading. Presser feet on older machines have a large thumb screw or need a screwdriver for removal.

Swing-out feet make it easier to change or thread needles. The foot pivots away from the needle. When the foot is in the "swing out" position the machine will not run. ►

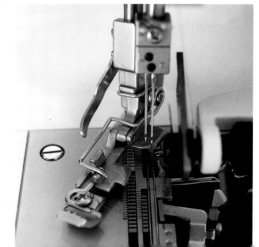

1-10

Some all-purpose presser feet (the foot that comes on the machine) will have a built-in cording or taping feature, and grooves, dots, or ridges for reference and guiding help. ▶

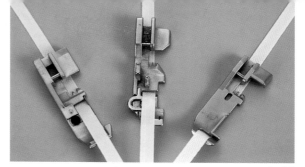

1-11

The presser foot lifter raises and lowers the presser foot. It may be located behind the presser foot on the back of the machine, in the cut-out area to the right of the needle, or on the right side of the machine above the handwheel. On many models, the presser foot can be raised higher by lifting the presser foot lifter more than the preset setting. This allows extra thick or bulky fabrics to be inserted under the presser foot. For a good serging technique, the presser foot lifter is used rarely, except when serging unusual fabrics, using decorative threads or trying an unconventional technique. ▶

Feed Dogs - The serger feed dogs serve the same function as those on the sewing machine, to help fabric travel under the presser foot. However, serger feed dogs are much longer, larger, and higher. Because of these differences, fabric moves easily and swiftly under the presser foot, at almost three times the speed that most people sew.

1-12

Knives - The knives are one of the most appreciated parts of a serger as they trim off extra fabric for a clean finish. There are two knives or blades positioned in front of the needle. The lower knife is stationary; the upper knife moves, usually up and down against the lower knife, creating a scissor-like cutting motion. Some upper knives are secured above the needle plate, and can be easily rolled up out of the way so as not to cut. Other upper knives are hook-shaped and secured next to the lower knife. This style knife may not allow the blade to be moved to a non-cutting position. ▶

1-13

The blades are made of strong, hard carbide steel and will last a long time when treated properly. Keep the blades free of dust and lint, and make sure that the knives and pins never meet. The knives will cut through pins, but it will be the last thing they will cut! When the knife begins to dull, the cut fabric edge will be ragged, rather than smooth and clean. You will first notice this on lightweight knits and woven fabrics. An extra lower blade usually comes with the machine. Replacement directions can be found in the instruction manual.

A recent, welcome addition to serger technology allows the lower knife to move side-to-side creating different stitch widths and better stitch quality. Consult your instruction manual for the location of this control.

Needle Plate and Stitch Finger - The smooth metal plate under the presser foot is the needle plate. It has a cut-out, rectangular-shaped area surrounding the feed dogs. You can see the feed dogs move in these openings. The stitch finger is part of the needle plate. It provides support for the threads as the stitch is forming. Some machines have more than one needle plate that must be changed for different stitch formations. Others have a lever, dial, or slide switch that adjusts the stitch finger width.

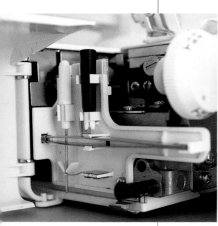

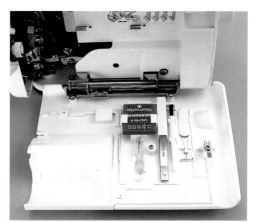

1-14   1-15   1-16

▲ **Accessories** - Helpful serger accessories, from tweezers to extra needles, are often stored inside the looper doors and in an extra pouch. Be sure to replace the accessories after using them so they are always available at your fingertips.

Needles

Sergers use from one to three needles depending on the selected stitch formation. Using the correct type, brand, and size needle is essential for perfect stitch quality and proper operation of your machine. Needles must be changed periodically, their life expectancy depends on the fabric and thread being serged.

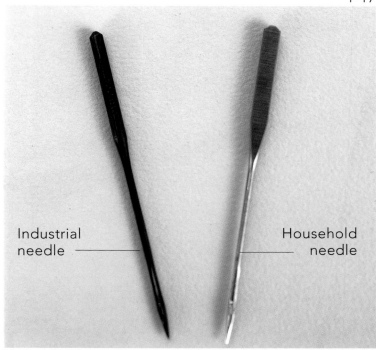

Industrial needle ——————

—————— Household needle

Your instruction manual will tell you what needle system your serger uses. The system is identified by industry recognized code numbers, such as 13O x 7O5H or DBxl, which name the needle. Most sergers today use regular "household" needles, the same type used in sewing machines. Older models may call for industrial needles. The two systems **are not** interchangeable, as they are usually of different length and diameter. Literature suggests that industrial needles are more durable than household ones. Testing and experience seems to indicate that there is not a significant difference for most personal-use sergers. Your serger may have its own brand of needles and it is a good practice to use that brand needle in your machine.

Industrial needles have a round shank; the household needle ▶ has one flat side. When inserting a household needle, the flat side of the shank is to the back. When inserting the industrial needle, take extra care that the long groove, the cut-out path for the thread, is toward the front and the eye of the needle is perfectly centered, front to back. A needle insertion tool to hold the needle or a T-pin inserted in the needle eye can help to align the needle.

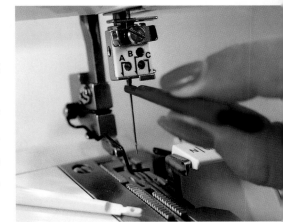

1-18

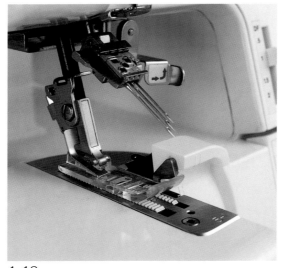

1-19

Also, be sure that the needle is "up" as far as it will go. This may be tricky to judge, as with the basic 4-thread stitch formation, the right needle is slightly longer than the left one.

◄ One model has a needle clamp that flips "up" for easier needle insertion.

Needles are held "in" with pressure from one or two tiny set screws located on the needle bar. Each needle may each have its own screw and insertion hole, or they may have different screws but a single hole. If the hole is shared, the right needle screw may have to be loosened to insert or remove the left needle. Good serging technique dictates that when a needle is not being used, it should be removed and the screw holding it tightened.

As a general rule, match the needle type and fabric being serged. Universal, semi-ballpoint needles will work satisfactorily with a large percentage of fabrics.

1-20

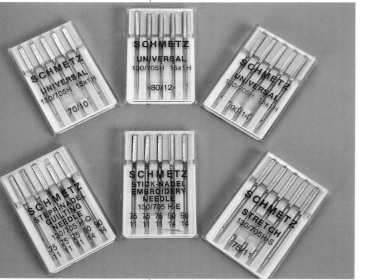

However, stitch quality on some wovens may improve by using a sharp, and on knits, a ballpoint needle. The most important rule to remember is that the needle should be in perfect condition with no burrs or dings, and it is not bent or damaged in any way.

◄ Unusual fabrics, creative techniques, or decorative threads may require the use of specialized needles. These include topstitch/jeans needles for very heavy fabrics or threads, or when using multiple strands of thread. They have a large, sharp point that cuts through the heavy fabric and a large eye to accommodate the thicker threads. Needles designed for use with metallic and novelty threads are referred to as embroidery needles and are very helpful in reducing thread breakage, shredding, and fraying. This needle has a large coated eye and deep groove that decreases abrasion on the thread. A special quilting needle is recommended when using batting of any kind. It is very sharp and will not damage the batting.

For most serging projects, the best results are achieved by using needle sizes #70, #80, and #90. These numbers correlate to the diameter of the needle; the larger the number, the larger the needle. A needle size smaller than #70 may not allow stitch formation. Anything larger than a #90 may cause serious mechanical damage because the needle may hit the loopers. An occasional technique may demand a needle out of this size range, but test first, by turning the handwheel manually and listening for any sound that indicates that the needle is hitting something.

There is not a set formula on how frequently to change the serger needles. It depends on what fabric is being serged — a synthetic fabric with a lot of finish or a fabric with metallic threads will dull a needle faster than a natural fabric. If you are experiencing small tension problems and nothing seems to remedy the situation, the cause is probably a dull needle. A dull needle results in skipped or partially formed stitches. A punching sound, suggesting that the needle is not gliding through the fabric, tells you the point is damaged or dull. Listen to your machine — it will tell you when it's time to change a needle.

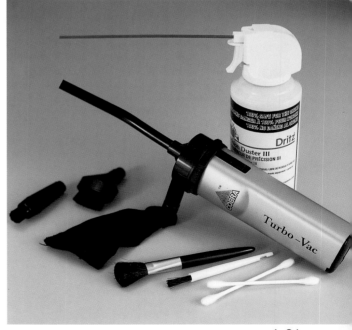

1-21

Serger Tools - Traditional and Some Surprises

Cleaning Tools - The nicest thing that can be done ▶ to a serger is to keep it clean and oiled. A machine full of lint from cut fabric will not perform at its very best. One helpful tool is a small mini-vacuum designed for cleaning photographic or computer equipment. A variety of small brushes can clean hard-to-reach areas. Consult your instruction manual for the frequency and location of oiling points. Be sure to use good-quality sewing machine oil on your serger.

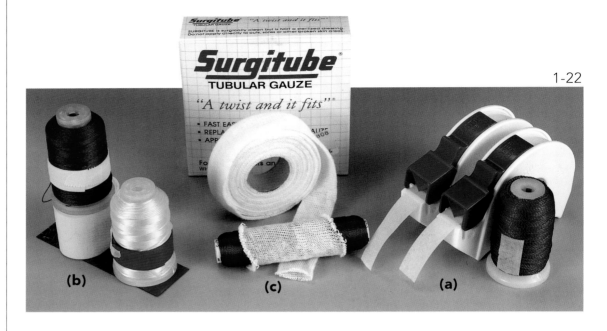

1-22

▲ **Thread Tapes** - Yards and yards of all-purpose and decorative serger thread can be lost when the threads are stored. The valuable threads, especially rayon, slide right off the spools. Use cloth or paper first-aid tape (a) or a tennis grip tape (b) to secure the thread ends. Surgitube (c), a gauze tubular bandage used on fingers, is perfect for covering an entire spool.

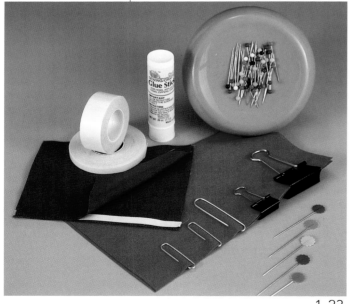

1-23

◄ **Fabric Securers** - There are numerous methods for holding the layers of fabric together when serging. They range from super-sized pins that are placed parallel and 1" - 2" away from the edge of the fabric, to glue sticks and double-sided tape. An office supply store yields different types of paper clips.

Tweezers - Thread guides in small, hard-to-reach places make tweezers an essential tool. A pair always comes with the machine but there are many other shapes and styles of tweezers available. Hemostats (a) and locking tweezers (b) provide a firm grip for threading needles and loopers. Check electronic and medical supply stores for a variety of shapes and sizes perfect for serging. ▶

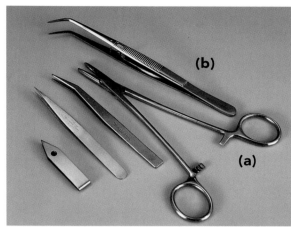
1-24

Bodkins - Bodkins are the proper name for giant needles. They are extremely helpful when threading elastic through casings or a serger thread tail back through the stitch. Some of these needles are actually called bodkins (a), others tapestry needles (b) or children's needles (c). ▶

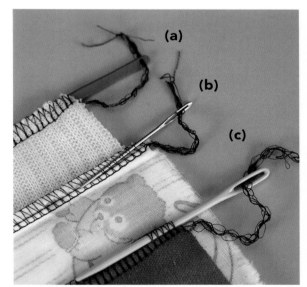
1-25

Needle Threaders - Serger needles are not only placed in a cramped, awkard position, but their eyes seem even smaller than on the sewing machine! Don't let mature eyesight make threading more difficult. Needle threaders come in many shapes and styles; try them all to find the best one for you. ▶

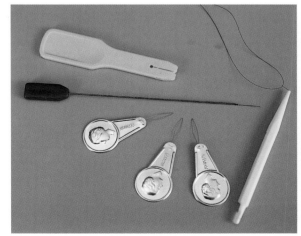
1-26

THREADS, THREADS, AND MORE THREADS

Thread is to a serger as gasoline is to a car. Different brands and qualities cause different results. Sometimes the car motor (or serger) will run smoothly, no strange noises or problems. Then, suddenly, there is something wrong. The car engine may stall (poor tension or stitch quality), or even die completely (threads break), all because the wrong "fuel" was used. This chapter provides thread information to help you make the right choice for the easiest "trip" to serging success.

Threads

As serger technology has advanced so has the availability of different kinds of thread. They vary in quality, form and size of packaging, weight, and type. Knowledge of thread differences, their strengths and weaknesses, and their designated use will allow you to make the best choice and save hours of troubleshooting time later.

Thread Quality or There's No Such Thing as a Bargain

You may think that a magnifying glass or a microscope is needed to determine the quality of the thread. This is not the case. Most often it's the price that gives the quality away! Bargain prices may mean poor quality and many headaches while serging later.

Good quality thread will be smooth and even, with few fibers "sticking out" from the core. It is made from fiber strands 5 1/2" - 6 1/2" in length, tightly spun or woven together. Inferior thread will have shorter fibers, from 1 1/2" - 2 1/2" in length. Long fiber, or, technically speaking, long staple thread will be stronger and easier to use. It will not have weak spots, knots, or slubs that result in uneven thread circumference. If the thread shape is irregular as it passes through the tension disks, it causes uneven tension or breakage from the abrasion of the thread guides and needle eyes. Valuable serger time may then have to be spent rethreading rather than serging. So, when selecting thread, choose with quality not price in mind.

Thread Packaging

Thread is sold in three basic forms: 1) a parallel-wound spool, 2) a cross-wound tube or spool, or 3) a cone.

1. The parallel-wound spool is the type sewers have used for many years. It's often referred to as "American thread." Some of us have vintage collections of these empty wooden spools. Save these old wooden spools — they are now made of plastic! ▶

2-1

Parallel-wound spools are designed so the thread feeds from the side of the spool, perfect for most sewing machines. However, the serger stitches at a much higher speed than the sewing machine and is designed to perform best using thread that feeds from the top of the spool. ▶

2-2

Parallel-wound thread can be used on the serger but a spool cap is often necessary. The spool cap keeps the thread from catching on the thread "notch" on one end of the spool and holds the spool on the thread stand. ▶

2-3

2. The cross-wound tube or spool is serger friendly. To identify it, look for a diamond-like pattern of thread on the spool. ▶

2-4

THREADS
THREADS
AND MORE
THREADS

2-5

◄ The thread feeds smoothly off the top of the spool, even when serging at a very high speed.

This thread should not need a spool cap. If the thread is very fine or slippery, it occasionally slides off the spool while it "stands up" on the thread holders. Place it on the table behind the machine. This will help prevent the sliding and keep the thread from wrapping around the spool pin. Preventative measures such as this save rethreading time and possible mechanical damage to the machine.

◄ **3**. Cone thread is the easiest, most economical way to purchase serger thread. Cones are cross-wound and available in quantities of 2,000 to 10,000 yards. The more thread wound on a cone, the cost-per-yard or meter decreases. Your serger will save time, not thread, so large cones are the most convenient, trouble-free way to purchase and maintain your thread supply.

2-6

2-7

◄ Be sure to use the coneholders that come with the serger to prevent the cones from rattling and flying off the spool pins while serging at high speed. Super-size industrial cones, 10,000 yards plus, will not fit on the machine thread stand, so place them on the table behind the serger or use a portable thread stand.

Thread Weight - Unraveling the Code

The content of a spool of thread is found printed on the spool or the packaging. Following the fiber name are numbers such as 50/3 or 30/3. These numbers indicate the thickness of the thread and the number of plies or strands used to make it. These factors plus how tightly the plies are twisted together will determine the thread's durability and suitability for serging. ▶

2-8

The first number in the labeling refers to the size of the ply of thread used. Cotton thread uses an English numbering system; synthetic threads a metric system. Both systems use a standard measurement of how many yards or meters of thread are made from a certain amount of raw material. The resulting comparison is similar for both systems; the higher the number, the finer or lighter weight the thread.

The second number refers to how many plies or strands of thread are spun together. For 50/3 cotton thread, three plies of 50-weight thread are twisted together. The result is a very fine, lightweight embroidery thread with minimal strength and limited serger use. A 30/3 cotton thread means three plies of a heavier, 30-weight thread are twisted together making cordonnet, jeans, or top-stitching thread. These are strong, heavy threads, with limited serger use.

Both of these threads can be used successfully on the serger but will need some extra TLC. Knowing how to read the thread codes and interpret the numbers can save valuable time and expense. It may also reveal some serging and thread options that were not previously considered.

Thread Type - Polyester, Cotton or What???

Does choosing the correct content or type of thread need a degree in chemistry or a magic wand? It probably takes a little bit of both. Our grandmothers chose either cotton or silk thread, and probably cotton, because of the expense of silk thread. We have so many more options. The variety of fibers used to make threads have their strengths, weaknesses, appearances, and durability, all factors to be considered when selecting thread for your serging project.

For example, a polyester or cotton-covered polyester thread has the strength, minimal stretch and durability needed to hold a garment together; therefore choose it for construction. Need a delicate, smooth, shiny-edge finish for a washed silk scarf? An all-purpose, construction-type thread would work well, but the result would be dull and boring. Instead, choose a rayon embroidery thread, a beautiful thread that comes in radiant colors and has a wonderful luster. Fine rayon thread is weak, but that is not an important construction consideration as the edge-finish will not be stressed or pulled.

2-9

◄ A practical consideration should be made as to how the project or garment will be cleaned or laundered. Make sure the thread is compatible with its final care. Even though serging the edge of a tablecloth with exquisite, heavy rayon thread is fast and easy, it would be a shame if the tablecloth could only be used once because in laundering the thread frayed, or its color ran. Many decorative or novelty threads have care codes on the labels. Before starting your project, check the codes to be sure both fabric and thread washing, drying, and pressing temperatures are compatible.

Below is a list of the threads most often used on the serger. They are coded for your reference: 1) where they may be used on the machine: N - needles, UL - upper looper, and LL - lower looper; 2) thread content; and 3) typical form of packaging. This information is not meant to be the last and final word on these particular threads, but more as a starting point for you in understanding threads and your serger.

All-purpose thread

N, UL, LL ▶

Polyester, blends

Spools, tubes, cones

Most often used thread – very strong and durable – many colors offered – good quality essential – cross-wound cones easiest and most economical to use – used for construction, edge finishing, decorative work – no special cleaning or washing instructions.

2-10

Serger cone thread

N, UL, LL ▶

Polyester, blends

Cones

Easy and economical to use – slightly lighter weight than all-purpose thread – cross-wound – good quality essential – used for construction, edge finishing, decorative work.

2-11

All-purpose cotton thread

N, UL, LL ▶

Cotton

Spools, tubes, cones

Slightly weaker than synthetic and blends – rich colors, slight luster – good quality essential – used for construction, edge finishing, decorative work.

2-12

Monofilament or nylon thread   N, UL, LL   ▶

Nylon   Spools, cones

Transparent, almost invisible on fabric – available in clear and smoke color – variety of weights available, finer than all-purpose threads – strong – good quality essential, some are wiry and stiff, causing tension problems – limited construction use, helpful in decorative and finishing work – needs care when pressing or drying.

2-13

2-14

◀ Textured nylon   N, UL, LL

Nylon   Cones

Referred to as Woolly Nylon™ – Crimped, not twisted so thread will stretch – "fluffy," will cover fabric underneath, creates a satin-stitch look – available in wide range of colors, variegated, metallics – Double Woolly Nylon™, a heavier, thicker, stretchy thread available in limited colors – used in construction, edge finishing, decorative work – ideal for swimwear, leotards, baby items – washes beautifully – needs care when pressing.

Embroidery threads   N, UL, LL   ▶

Rayon, cotton, metallic   Spools, tubes, cones

Very fine, lightweight thread – limited strength and durability – varied, luxurious, bright colors – variegated and blended colors available – used for edge finishing, decorative work – rayon and metallic need care when washing and pressing.

2-15

Heavier rayon threads   UL, LL   ▶

Rayon   Cones, spools

Known as Decor, Decor 6, Designer 6, with little twist, also known as Pearl Crown Rayon, which is twisted – thicker, heavier thread – very shiny – many rich, vibrant colors – used for decorative work, edge finishing, flatlocking – care needed when wearing, washing, or cleaning.

2-16

Super-fine metallics   N, UL, LL   ▶

Synthetics, polymers   Spools

Known as Tinsel, Silver – very, very shiny – little strength – used for decorative application only – mixes well with other threads – needs care when pressing.

2-17

Heavier cotton thread   UL, LL   ▶

Cotton   Spools, cones, skeins

Includes pearl cotton, crochet threads, embroidery floss, cordonnet – many colors, variegated, some luster – good quality essential – results in thick heavy coverage – used for decorative work, edge finishing, flatlocking.

2-18

Heavy metallic threads UL, LL ▶

Synthetics, blends Tubes, cones

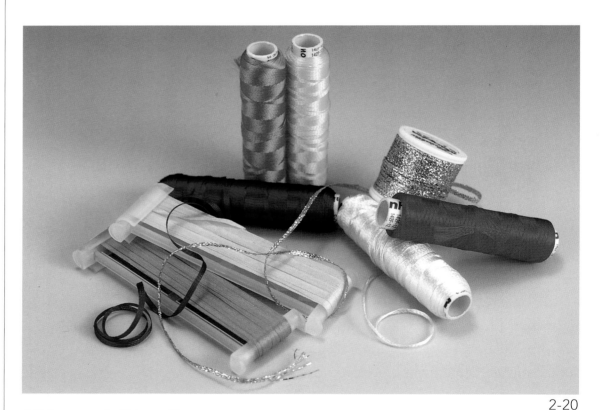

Candlelight, Glamour – variety of colors, mixed, variegated – adds glitz, sparkle – used for decorative work, edge finishing, flatlocking – care needed when wearing, cleaning, and pressing, depending on fiber content.

2-19

2-20

Ribbon and ribbon floss UL, LL ▲

Silk, rayon, polyester Spools, tubes, skeins

Ribbon specifically packaged for serger use, 1/16" wide – ribbon "by the yard" is generally too stiff and heavy, won't feed properly – rich, luxurious colors, metallics – used for decorative work, edge finishing, flatlocking – limited yardage in packaging – care needed when cleaning, depending on fiber content.

2-21

Yarns UL, LL ▶

Cotton, acrylic, wool, blends Tubes, skeins

Some yarns available with serger-friendly pack-▶
aging – very lightweight to 3-ply baby or sport yarn
most suitable – test for strength, some may be too
weak to resist abrasion and make it through the
machine – variety of colors, variegated – used for
decorative work, edge finishing, flatlocking – care
needed in cleaning depending on fiber – avoid
uneven yarn with "slubs" or lots of texture, won't
feed properly.

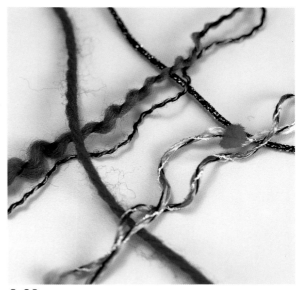
2-22

Fusible thread LL ▶

Polyester, polymer Cones, spools

A polyester thread wrapped with a fusible material –
acts as a bonding agent when activated by heat –
used to secure edges, hems, seams.

2-23

Should all serger threads match? Or do I really have to buy four or five spools of thread for everything I make?

The answer to both of these questions is a definite "depends." It's a matter of personal preference. Some people prefer to have all threads match, not only the ones on the serger, but the sewing machine, too. If you are that type, you do have to purchase multiple spools of the same color. However, if you are not of that ilk, here's some information to help you reduce the amount of thread you have to buy.

Thread is used more quickly on the loopers than on the needles. This makes sense as it takes more thread to make "loops" than to go in and out of the fabric. By exchanging spools, from looper to needle, and needle to looper, neither spool will completely run out requiring the purchase of additional thread.

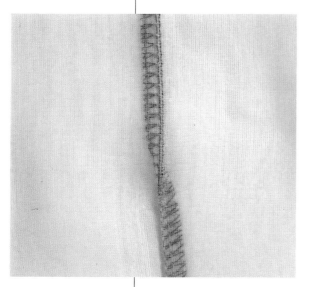

You can avoid buying additional spools by winding thread from large cones to sewing machine bobbins for use through the serger needles. This alternative may depend on the size of the project as bobbins hold relatively little thread and will empty very quickly when used on the serger. They are also not an ideal design for use on the serger because bobbins may not fit on the spool pin properly and spin or just not allow the thread to feed evenly. Again, it just "depends" on the situation.

Whether or not threads match the fabric also "depends" on which thread will show.

2-24

▲ If the fabric is lightweight and sheer, or the garment is to be viewed inside out, then it's more attractive to have threads match. But in many cases, only one, if any, thread shows.

When using the serger for seam construction, it's the needle thread that shows when the seam is pulled apart. If two needles are used, the left needle thread is visible. ▶

2-25

When finishing a hem, serge the edge with the right side of the fabric up. The upper looper thread will be the most obvious. It "depends" on how much the color differences bother you whether or not you change threads. ▶

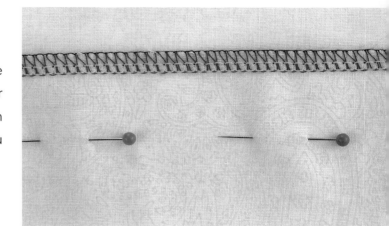

2-26

A pleasant compromise to the thread matching debate is to use blending threads. If you place a variety of fabrics, all colors and patterns, on a table and place different color threads with them you will discover that there are some "blenders," colors that seem to go with everything. The obvious ones are ivory or creme colors for light color fabrics, and grays for dark colors. Mauve, rose and light blue are also blenders. You may be happy to leave the "blenders" on the looper threads and match the needle thread. It just "depends" on what you want! ▶

2-27

WHICH STITCH IS WHICH??

At first glance, it appears that the serger can create only one stitch formation. However, with a choice of needles and loopers to use, and the variety of tension adjustments available, many additional options are revealed.

Focus on Basic Serger Stitch Formations

The following describes the basic serger stitch types. These basic stitches are referred to as the functional stitches. They may be altered for decorative or extraordinary seams or edge finishes. Examine the characteristics of each to choose the best stitch for your project.

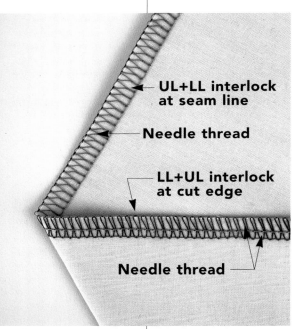

UL+LL interlock
at seam line

Needle thread

LL+UL interlock
at cut edge

Needle thread

3-1

◄ The serger stitch shown is a 4-thread formation. It differs from a sewing machine stitch in that there is no bobbin thread. Instead, there are loopers, designated as the upper and the lower looper. Looper threads interlock at the seam line and/or the cut edge with the needle threads forming the securing stitches. This gives the stitch a crocheted relationship rather than a locked one like a sewing machine stitch. The needle thread(s) penetrate through the fabric while the looper thread(s) lay on the fabric and are held in place by the needle thread(s). The crocheted relationship means that the stitch will "give" or stretch depending on the fabric serged. Used on interlock knit, lycra, fleece, or lingerie-type fabric, the serged seam will stretch with body movement, then miraculously recover or return to the original size. Used on a woven fabric, the seam will "give" or stretch slightly, building in a natural ease. A loosely woven, lightweight fabric like challis or linen will have much more "give" or stretch than a heavier, densely woven fabric like denim or twill.

The stitch formation selected will depend on: the fabric, the style and use of the finished product, and the location of the seam. Knowing the attributes of each stitch will allow you to make the best choice. Consult your instruction manual for the stitch formations that can be accomplished on your serger.

2-Thread Overlock Stitch

The 2-thread overlock stitch uses one needle and one looper. The needle and looper used is determined by the desired stitch width and the model of serger being used.

The two threads lock at the edge of the fabric, not at ▶ the seam line. This stitch does not make a traditional seam but pulls open and lies flat. In serger terms, it is a natural flatlock.

The 2-thread overlock stitch is an excellent edge finish, especially on sheer or lightweight fabrics. It uses less thread, and is not bulky or visible.

This stitch will result in a stretchy seam. On knit fabric, it will stretch both in the lengthwise and crosswise direction. It may not be a good choice for the main construction stitch on woven fabrics as the edges are not finished.

3-2

2-Thread Chainstitch

The 2-thread chainstitch is formed using one needle and one looper. Depending on the serger model, the looper used may be part of the overlock stitch mech- anism or designated solely for the chainstitch. The needle thread appears as a straight stitch on one side of the fabric, the looper thread forms small loops or a chain on the reverse side.

This stitch forms a traditional closed seam, like a sewing ▶ machine seam. When used alone, it does not provide a fin- ished edge. Depending on the fabric used, it will have little, if any, lengthwise stretch but significant crosswise stretch or ease. When heavy thread is used in the needle, the straight- stitch side of the chainstitch makes a heavy, pronounced

3-3

topstitch. The chainstitch is easily removed by pulling on the needle thread, making it a wonderful basting stitch.

By serging the chain alone, not into fabric, button or belt loops can be made. Use decorative threads for the chainstitch and create one-of-a-kind tassels, fringe, or other decorative trims.

3-4

◀ 3-Thread Overlock Stitch

The 3-thread overlock stitch is formed with one needle and two loopers. It is sometimes called an overedge stitch and is available on almost all personal-use sergers. This stitch will be 3mm - 7mm wide depending on whether the left or right needle is used.

The threads of a 3-thread overlock seam lock at the seam line and cut edge to form a strong durable seam. Technically, it is the seam providing the most stretch. When set for the widest stitch, it is the best choice for construction seams on most fabrics. In its narrower form, it can be used as the construction seam on lightweight fabrics in low stress areas.

The 3-thread overlock stitch is also ideal for edge finishing. With tension adjustment, this stitch becomes a rolled hem or flatlock stitch.

4-Thread Overlock Stitch

This stitch is formed using two needles and two loopers. It is called the 3-thread overlock with safety stitch. Depending on the brand and model of serger, this stitch will be between 5.5mm - 9mm wide.

Both of the needle threads interlock with the looper threads when forming the 4-thread overlock stitch, making it very strong and durable. It is perfect for construction seams on all fabric types. The advantage of having two needles is that if one needle thread breaks with wear the other will act as the safety stitch and still hold the seam together.

Though many believe the 4-thread overlock seam stretches less than a 3-thread overlock seam, the difference in stretch is slight. It is rarely necessary to use all four threads for edge finishing but on lofty, bulky fabrics, the four threads pack or condense the fabrics. By reducing the bulk, the fabric will feed more easily through the serger or the sewing machine. The resulting finished look may mean a garment that does not have to lined. ▶

3-5

WHICH
STITCH IS
WHICH?

3-6

4-Thread Safety Stitch

The 4-thread safety stitch formation has two parts, a chain-stitch forming a strong locked stitch at the seam line and a 2-thread overlock stitch as an edge finish.

◄ The chainstitch is formed with one chainstitch looper and one needle. The 2-thread overlock stitch uses one needle and one looper. The 4-thread safety stitch has minimal, if any, stretch or give lengthwise, but will stretch crosswise. It provides a strong seam, wider than a regular 3- or 4-thread overlock seam. It is the seam often used in ready-to-wear clothing and on home decorating items.

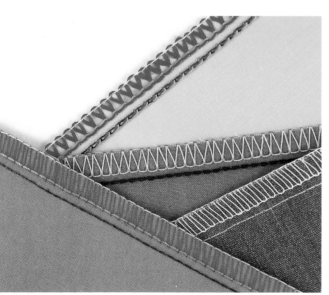

◄ 5-Thread Safety Stitch

The 5-thread safety stitch has similar characteristics to the 4-thread safety stitch, the difference being, the edge finishing stitch is a 3-thread overlock.

3-7

The stitch is formed with two needles and three loopers. The chainstitch requires one needle and one looper; the overlock stitch, one needle and two loopers. It provides the strongest, most stable seam, ideal for use with woven fabrics of all weights. There is minimal stretch or give lengthwise but some ease in the crosswise direction.

Cover Stitch or Cover Hem Stitch

Until recently, this stitch formation was available only on industrial machines. It is formed with two needles and a looper thread. Some machines dedicate separate needles and a looper for this stitch only. A specialized foot and flatbed insert or extension plate may also be needed.

The upper knife of a serger set for a cover stitch is raised or disengaged so there is no cutting action. The stitch appears to have two or three rows of parallel straight stitching, 3mm - 5mm apart, on the right side and a row of "loops" or an overlock-appearing stitch on the reverse side. You will immediately recognize it as the stitch used in ready-to-wear garments. ▶

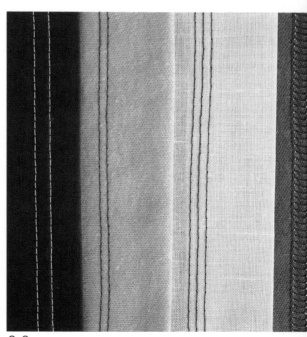

There is considerable stretch in this stitch. It has practical, functional, or decorative uses. Either side can be used as the right side. Decorative threads may be used in the needles and looper.

Recently, a separate machine was introduced to the home market which only does a cover stitch and chain stitch and has no knife for trimming.

3-8

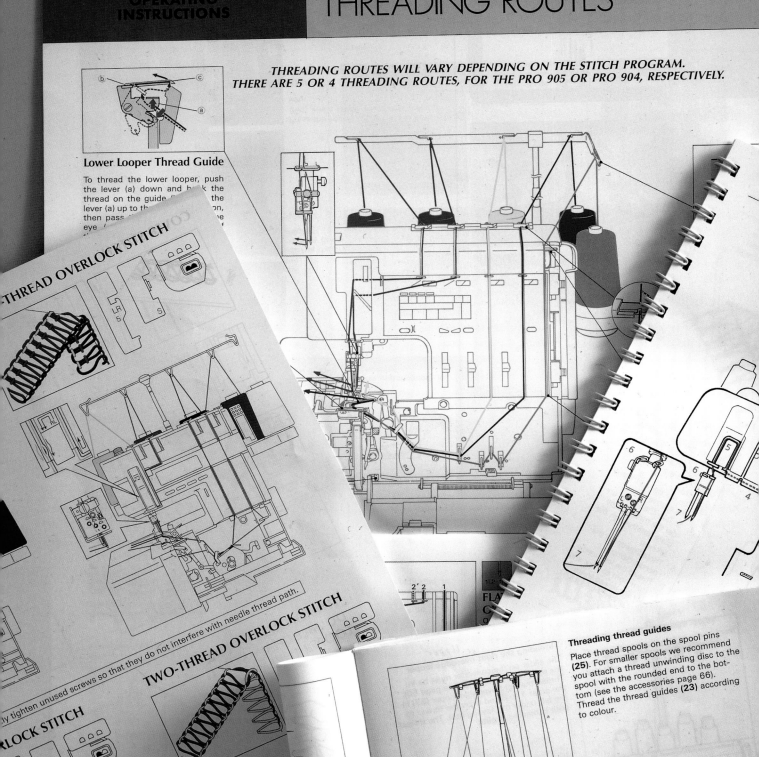

*THREADING ROUTES WILL VARY DEPENDING ON THE STITCH PROGRAM.
THERE ARE 5 OR 4 THREADING ROUTES, FOR THE PRO 905 OR PRO 904, RESPECTIVELY.*

Lower Looper Thread Guide

To thread the lower looper, push the lever (a) down and back the thread on the guide. the lever (a) up to the position, then pass the eye

THREE-THREAD OVERLOCK STITCH

TWO-THREAD OVERLOCK STITCH

tighten unused screws so that they do not interfere with needle thread path.

LOCK STITCH

50

Threading thread guides

Place thread spools on the spool pins **(25)**. For smaller spools we recommend you attach a thread unwinding disc to the spool with the rounded end to the bottom (see the accessories page 66). Thread the thread guides **(23)** according to colour.

THREADING AND RETHREADING

It's finally time to thread your serger! The thought of threading a serger pushes some people to the brink of a panic attack. They have heard horror stories about the time it takes to thread a serger, the frustration of having threads break, and the "lower looper nightmare." As is the case with many machines, it works much better when you follow directions! It's also helpful to have the correct tools and use some helpful tricks and tips.

THREADING
AND
RETHREAD-
ING

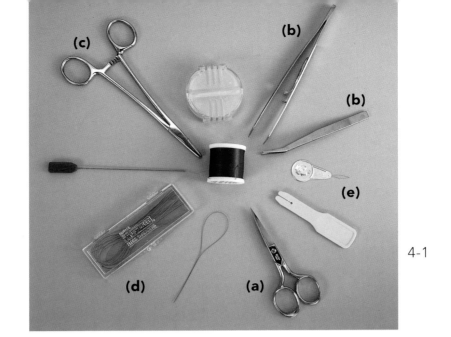

4-1

▲ Prepare to thread the serger by collecting helpful tools. Essential ones include sharp scissors (a) to cut thread ends and tweezers (b) to pull or aim threads through thread guides. Other helpful tools include hemostats (c), locking tweezers that hold the thread "in" the tweezer-like tool, Butler dental floss threaders (d) that will make threading looper eyes effortless, and a needle threader (e) to help combat mature eye sight!

First, prepare the serger to be threaded by making sure the thread pole is extended to its highest position. The top part must be turned in the correct direction. There is an arrow or marking that indicates "this way forward." The thread base of some sergers moves left and right to fit into a case or for use with different stitch formations; it must be locked in the correct position.

4-2

◄ Adjust all tensions to the middle of their suggested range. Some literature suggests that all tensions be set to zero, or the no tension setting for threading. The problem with this is remembering where the tensions were set and getting them reset when threading is finished. This middle range area is usually highlighted on the dial or disk. When a serger sets the tension for you, or suggests a tension on an LED screen, take its suggestion.

Next, open the front looper cover and side door. This will offer greater visibility and more light in the looper area. If your machine allows it, roll the knife up out of the way. You may also want to raise, then remove, the presser foot to allow more room for fingers and threading tools. On some machines raising the presser foot releases the tension so the tension disks or slides can be easily threaded. Even if the tension is not released it is a good threading habit.

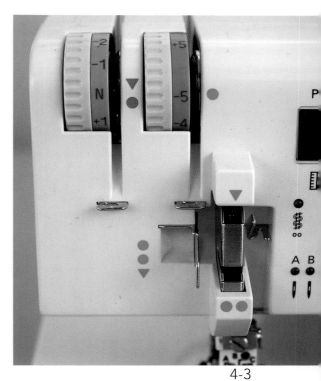

After placing the thread on the spool holders, begin threading following the threading paths. The codes may be symbols, colors, or both coded. When learning to thread, match the color of the thread to the colored dots or other marking used. If you experience tension or stitch quality problems, it is helpful to return to this color-coded thread to find the problem. ▶

Few things in the sewing and serging world have unconditional, must-be-followed rules. The sequence and manner of threading a serger may be as close as it gets. Threading must be done according to the sequence given for that machine. Every thread guide must be threaded or stitch quality will be compromised.

4-3

The only exception to this rule is with a machine with a pneumatic or Jet-Air™ threading system. These machines may be threaded in any order. Thread ends are barely pushed into threading "ports" and are sucked through the machine. All the guides, including the eye of the loopers, are threaded. ▶

4-4

THREADING
AND
RETHREAD-
ING

The typical threading sequence for a 4-thread overlock stitch is upper looper, lower looper, right needle, left needle. Variation from this sequence makes the serger more difficult to thread because thread guides become covered or hard to reach.

It is important to take extra care when threading the tension slots or dials. With slotted tension you can see the two tension disks side-by-side. Be sure that the thread is securely between the disks, not sitting on top of them. ▶

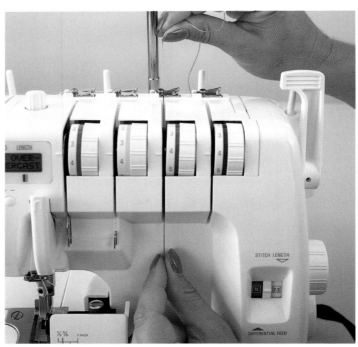

4-5

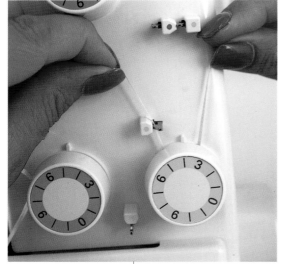

4-6

◀ To lock the thread onto tension dials, pull the thread between the disks in a flossing-type motion. In either case, you should feel a slight pull or resistance on the thread when the thread is seated properly.

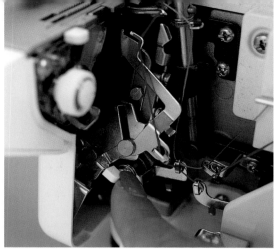

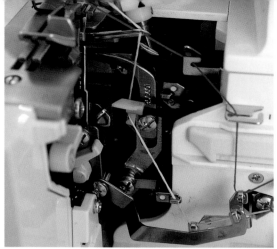

4-7 4-8

The dreaded lower looper is the next challenge in threading. Newer- ▲
model machines have a variety of lower looper threading systems. This may be
the most important time to consult your instruction manual. It will explain the
location and operation of this priceless helper. If you must thread the lower
looper unaided, try threading the eye of the looper first, then pulling the thread
to the hard-to-reach left-end thread guide of the lower looper. However, this
may not always be possible. Sometimes the left-end thread guide of the looper
is closed and must be threaded.

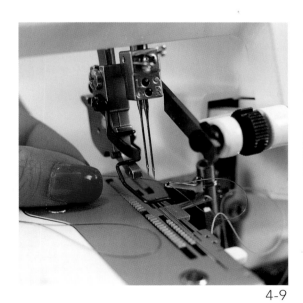

4-9 4-10

Next, be sure that all thread guides are threaded. Most machines have ▲
open guides and thread may be easily slipped into place. If guides are closed,
hidden, or just difficult to reach, your tweezers, Butler dental floss threader, dental mirror, or looper threader will be very helpful when guiding the thread.

THREADING
AND
RETHREAD-
ING

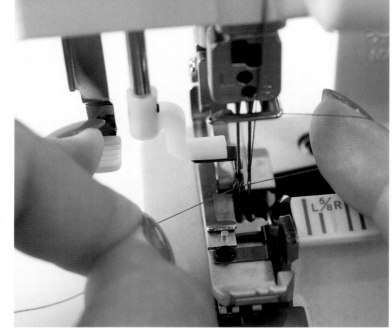

4-11

4-12

▲ The needle(s) are threaded last. Again, be sure that the threads are securely in the tension disks or slots. On many sergers, needle threads share thread guides and are separated just above the needles.

◄ There is very little space around the needle for fingers. Use tweezers to aim the thread at the eye of the needle. Any sewing machine needle threader will be greatly appreciated in this case.

4-13

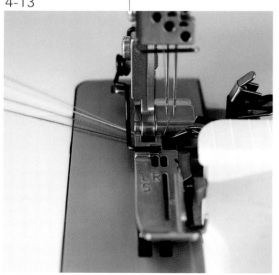

◄ When threading is complete all threads should be placed under the presser foot and positioned to the "10 o'clock position."

N (Needles) ▶

Is the needle inserted correctly?

Is the correct size and type of needle being used?

Is the needle blunt, bent, or damaged?

4-22

T (Tension) ▶

Understanding serger tension can be the most confusing, but a most important skill to have when using a serger. The following chapter will provide you with the full explanation.

The **TNT** formula will solve 85% - 95% of your stitch quality problems. Your investigation should always follow the sequence given: **T** - threading, **N** - needles, and **T** - tension. It is understandable that if the machine is not threaded properly, adjustments in the other areas will make little difference. Also, if the needle is not sharp and straight, tension adjustments will do little, if anything, to improve stitch quality.

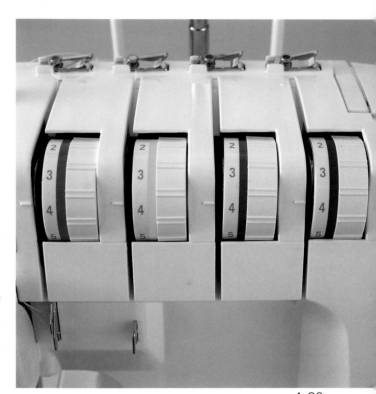

4-23

Using **TNT** will save time, and wear and tear on the operator's nerves, and maybe even the serger itself, because it will not be hurled out the closest window when it misbehaves!

Threading Shortcuts or the "Really Easy" Way to Thread a Serger

▼ Now that you are familiar with every idiosyncrasy of threading your serger, it's time to reveal the "easy" way. Some serger teachers call this cheating, but using this method just makes good use of your serging time!

When the upper or lower looper thread needs to be changed, those threads may be easily "tied on." Cut off the old thread just above the spool. Place the new thread on the spool pin and tie it to the old thread with a simple overhand knot. Pull the threads apart to check to see if the knot is secure. Carefully trim off any thread tail longer than 2"-3."

These new threads can either be gently pulled or serged through the machine. If the threads are to be pulled through, some TLC for your serger is necessary.

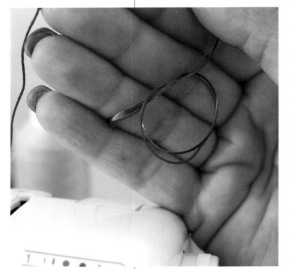

4-24

If the tension on the serger can be released by raising the presser foot or in some other manner, do it! It saves wear and tear on the tension disks. If the tension is not released automatically when the foot is raised, you can turn all the tension disks to the lowest number.

After "tying-on," gently pull the looper threads ONLY through the serger until the knots appear past the eye of the loopers. If the thread seems to catch, STOP, do not force it. Examine the threading trail to see where it's caught. If you continue to force the thread, you take a chance of bending or breaking a looper or thread guide.

There are two ways to serge the new looper threads through the machine. One way is to hold on to the thread tail and gently pull it while you run the serger. The other is to serge on a piece of fabric until the knot appears.

If the needle thread(s) must be changed, treat it as you would your sewing machine needle thread. Clip the thread just above the eye of the needle. Draw the old thread out "backwards," pulling from the spool end of the thread. Then rethread the needle. Although possible, it is not recommended to pull the needle thread through the machine. More than likely the knot won't go through the eye of the needle, so threading the eye is still necessary. Pulling on the needle thread while it's threaded may bend the needle. The needle will hit the needle plate of the machine while you are serging and break, or it may clear the plate, but hit a looper inside the machine. Hitting the looper could cause serious mechanical or timing problems.

The "tie-on" method of rethreading won't work every time. The key to its success is if the knot joining the two threads will fit through the eye of the looper. When changing from one all-purpose thread to the other or using any lightweight thread, there should be no problem. However, if a heavier decorative thread is introduced, the knot will be larger and may not fit. Avoid serging the thread through the machine. Instead, gently pull it through until the knot meets the eye of the looper. Cut the thread, and thread the eye. It takes slightly more time, but it's better than starting from scratch! It's wise not to take any shortcuts here. Forcing the thread knot to go through the looper will, at best, break the thread and, at worst, bend or break loopers.

Note: The consequences of threading and rethreading incorrectly may sound severe. They rarely are, but the possibility exists. The rules and suggestions offered are good serger technique and habit, and will save frustration and prevent you the inconvenience of having a "sick" serger later.

TAKE THE TENSION OUT OF TENSION THEORY

An overlock machine has three to five tension adjustments, one for each thread. Does this mean it will give the operator three to five tension headaches? Not at all. When explained step-by-step, serger tension theory is a logical, easy-to-understand concept. The fear and intimidation associated with serger tension adjustment probably is derived from many novice stitchers being threatened with amputation of their fingers if they ever touched the tension on their sewing machine! That is not the case with the serger. Tension is adjusted to maintain stitch quality, to change stitch formations, and the best part, to create. So, put the fears aside and quiet the "do not touch the tension" voices from the past. True serger confidence will come with the understanding of tension theory.

Tension: A Definition

Mechanically (and the serger is a machine, though on occasion it can have an attitude of its own), tension is the stretching or pulling of something. Most often the stretch is longitudinal, or lengthwise. In the case of the serger, it's threads that are being stretched. The amount of stretch determines how much thread is allowed through the machine and into the overlock stitch. A small amount of stretch – low or loose tension – means more thread is allowed through the machine. A large amount of stretch – high or tight tension – allows less thread through the serger. The key will be that the amount of thread moving through each position is balanced or in proportion to the others. Then, the desired result can be achieved.

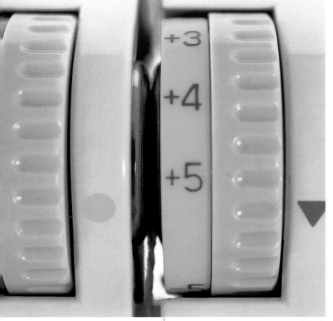

5-1

Tension Knobs, Dials, and Slides

◄ The tension mechanism on a serger is two disks positioned very close together, parallel to each other. Each thread has its own tension control. Hidden heavy springs provide pressure or resistance between the disks. The amount of pressure allows varying amounts of thread through the machine. Adjustment of the tension, of the change in the pressure of the springs, is accomplished in a variety of ways.

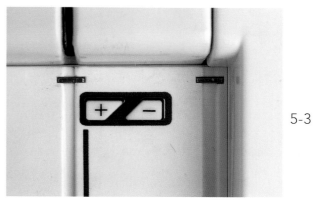

5-2

5-3

▲ The tension settings are changed using dials, knobs, or slides, depending upon the make and model of the machine. Located on or near the tension controls is some kind of symbolic reference system. Dials are numbered from 0-9, or have a plus "+" or minus "-" indication. The higher the number, or the more to the plus "+" side, the greater the tension being exerted on the thread. Newer, user-friendly machines have dials that turn one revolution. Earlier serger models have no numerical or symbol indication and dials can be turned as many as nineteen times! When the correct stitch was found, it is rarely changed!

Slide switches can have the same numerical or "+" and "-" indications, and are moved up and down. Some new top-of-the-line sergers automatically set tensions when a stitch formation is selected. The tension can be fine-tuned with slide switches or a numerical system. ▶

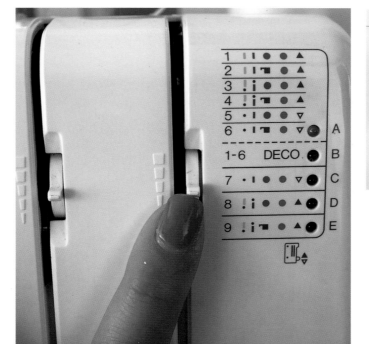

5-4

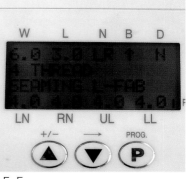

5-5

It must be stressed that whatever the system, numerical or "+" or "-", it's for reference and comparison only. Two of the same make and model machines may have entirely different settings and still achieve a perfect overlock stitch. One machine may have to be adjusted two numbers for a stitch formation change and the other only one. This is known as machine personality. Sewing machines have personalities too, but they do not seem as varied as sergers.

The Perfect Overlock Stitch

When learning serger tension theory, it is easiest to examine the 4-thread overlock stitch. This stitch should be tested using two layers of medium-weight fabric prepared for a seam. Stitch length and cutting width should be set in their normal range (SL: 2 - 2.5 mm and CW slightly less than 2). Other stitch formations are variations of this one so an understanding of its structure, form, and tensions will transfer to other stitches. Consider threading the serger with different colors of thread to match the threading symbols or path, then a problem thread can be easily identified.

The perfect 4-thread overlock stitch will have a left needle thread that, from the top side, travels smoothly and uniformly from loop to loop. With matching threads, it is difficult to tell where the looper thread and the needle threads meet. On the under side, it will also be smooth and uniform and look very much like a sewing machine stitch. When the seam is pulled open, it is the left needle thread that shows, just slightly, as with a sewing machine seam.

On the top side of the fabric, the right needle thread will appear very much like the left needle with the line of stitching traveling approximately half way between the left needle thread and the loops. On the under side, however, the right needle thread will appear as a tiny loop around the lower looper thread. It will sometimes appear to be looser than the left needle, but unless the looseness is exaggerated, it is sound. In the correctly balanced 4-thread formation, the right needle is the safety stitch and is barely visible on the wrong side of a seam, and not seen at all when the seam is pulled open. ▶

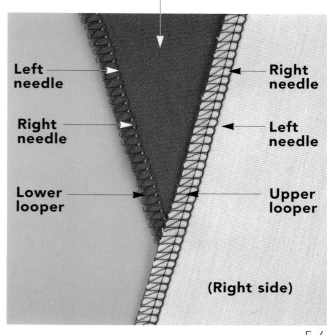

5-6

Needle tension problems reveal themselves at the seam line and are exhibited in two ways. One, if either of the needle threads appears to form loops or be loose, or a seam pulls apart, the tension is allowing too much thread through the machine. In this case, the tension must be increased or tightened. If either or both tensions are too tight and not allowing enough thread through the machine, then the seam will pucker, or in the worst case the thread will break when pulled flat. The tension must be loosened or decreased to solve the problem. ▶

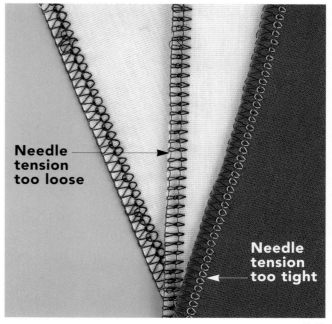

5-7

TAKE THE TENSION OUT OF TENSION THEORY

The looper threads should lay flat on the fabric, their loops interlocking on the seam line with the needle threads and with each other on the cut edge. When

looking at the top side of the stitch, the entire upper looper thread can be seen and the lower looper "loop" will be just barely visible on the cut edge. The reverse is true when examining the underside of the stitch.

5-8

◄ If a looper tension is too loose it will be pulled to the other side of the fabric. So, if the upper looper thread is too loose, the lower looper thread will pull it around the cut edge to the under side. They will not meet on the edge. When the lower looper is loose, it is pulled to the top side.

◄ Similar problems will occur if a tension is too tight. A too-tight upper looper will pull a lower looper around to the top side; a tight lower looper will result in upper looper threads being pulled to the under side.

Determining which thread is too tight or too loose has a semi-logical process, but it is more often trial and error. Generally, work first with the thread that appears to be to loose, as it is easier to see!

5-9

The Not-So-Perfect Overlock Stitch

Variations from "perfect" tension can be caused by everything from the weather (humidity and barometric pressure affecting the thread) to the color of the thread (the amount of dye used). Factors such as how soon the project being serged must be finished – the rush factor – or whether the machine operator has his/her mouth open or closed, and many things in between can also cause variations! The machine operator has no control over some of the factors and total command over others. The causes of and solutions to problems due to mechanical changes are manageable and are examined next; other problems may need divine intervention!

Some tension problems are minor and may not be visible without a magnifying glass. The need for adjustment will depend on whether or not a perfectionist is pushing on the foot control. Following are some areas to examine before serger frustration becomes intolerable.

TNT

The **T** - Threading; **N** - Needle; **T** - Tension formula (dis- ▶ cussed in Chapter 4) will solve 85% - 95% of serger problems. Check these things first! Missing a seemingly unimportant thread guide is a possible cause for serger "hiccups." This looks like a tension problem and shows up in the looper thread. The stitch quality is irregular, but in a pattern. Check the threading path carefully, but also examine the spool or cone of thread. Is the thread caught on a notch or other rough area of the spool? Perhaps the thread is catching on a spot as it comes off the cone. The key is that poor stitch quality has a rhythm. If no cause for the hiccups can be discovered, change the thread! A new spool or cone, or even moving it to a new location may be the cure!!

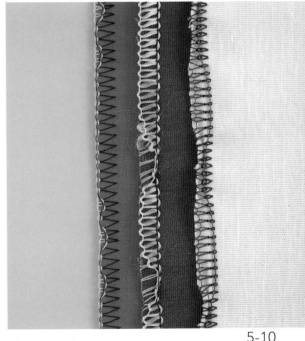

5-10

TAKE THE
TENSION
OUT OF
TENSION
THEORY

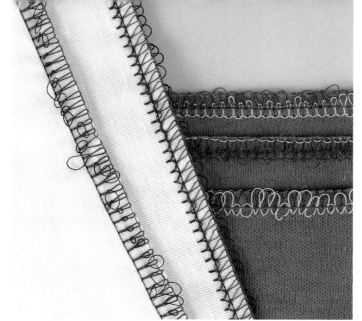

5-11

▲ Large loops of any one of the threads mean that the serger is allowing too much thread through and hiccups have become burps! Check to be sure that each thread is seated properly in the tension disks. Floss the disks, being sure thread is between them. Sometimes it may be necessary to turn the tension to its lowest setting so the disks offer the least resistance while threading, but don't forget to put them back or the stitch appearance may remain the same.

Thread Type

Different thread types, with their varying properties, will need different tension consideration. The following comments are suggestions and guidelines, not absolutes.

Thicker, heavier threads will need less tension because, with their larger circumference, they take up more space between the tension disks. Too much tension will impede thread progress through the machine and there won't be enough thread to make the stitch.

Very fine cotton or poly/cotton threads may need more tension to hold them back and prevent too much thread from going into the stitch. However, if the thread is shiny or slippery, such as a rayon or rayon blend, it could have some inherent stretch and need less tension.

Some decorative and novelty threads have a great deal of texture. They are not smooth and even. They offer their own resistance so will need far less tension than an all-purpose thread. They may be so uneven that they will be unsuitable for use in the serger. The best example of this would be a slubbed or knotted yarn. Some specialty threads, like textured nylon or elastic thread, are meant to stretch. They will need a lower, looser tension so not to stretch too much and pucker the seam when they relax..

Some threads offer a combination of all these qualities. The only way to find the correct tension for them is to ....**TEST, TEST, TEST.**

Fabric Weight

The weight or thickness of the fabric ▶ being serged may influence tension settings. To understand this, visualize a piece of lightweight fabric, such as batiste, as a piece of paper, and middleweight, calico-type fabrics as twenty sheets of paper. A small paperback book represents denim and lighter weight drapery fabric, and a dictionary is fake fur, tapestry, or bulky fleece, or velour. Picture the amount of looper thread it would take to encircle each piece. The thicker the paper product or fabric, the more thread it will take. If more thread is needed, the tension must be looser, or lower.

5-12

Stitch Length

Average or normal stitch length for a 4-thread overlock stitch is 2mm - 2.5mm. Most often the tension will be balanced to this stitch length. However, changes in stitch length, especially extreme ones, will warrant tension changes.

The tension adjustments may be needed in the needles, the loopers, or all threads. If the symptom is the loops, there is too much thread, so tighten the tension. If there is puckering or threads are not meeting at the edge, there is too little thread, so loosen the tension.

5-13

◄ Stitch length is the measurement of the distance between needle penetrations. At 2.5mm, the needle goes into the fabric every 2.5mm, and so forth. The longer or father apart the stitches are, the more thread it takes to make the stitch. At a stitch length of 4mm, more thread must go into the stitch, so the tension, especially looper tension, may need to be loosened. At a short stitch length, far less thread is needed because the needle penetrations are close together. Tensions may need to be tightened or increased to allow less thread into the stitch.

Stitch Width

Left & right needle

Right needle only

5-14

◄ Stitch width is determined by which needle is used and the cutting width setting. Both of these regulate how far the cut edge of the fabric is from the needle. The difference in width is obvious when changing needles. The change made when adjusting the cutting width is not as visible, but is the adjustment needed to fine tune the stitch to perfection. If a tension adjustment is needed, it will be in the looper tension, as it will take a different amount of thread to allow the threads to meet at the edge of the fabric.

Picture a wide stitch as being a quilting ruler, the narrow one as being a yard stick. It will take more thread (less tension) to reach from side to side of the quilting ruler than the yard stick. The same is true with fabric. ▶

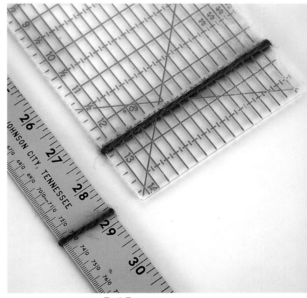

5-15

When a machine has a cutting width adjustment available, also called the stitch width, the operator has a choice. One option is to readjust the tension. The other, often easier option, is to fine tune the cutting width. If there appears to be too little looper thread and the seam is cupping (a) or rolling up under the stitch (b), cut off more fabric. Depending on the machine, this means lowering the cutting width. If the loops are off the cut edge (c), too much fabric is being cut off, so raise the cutting width setting to cut off less fabric. ▶

The need to make this adjustment is sometimes revealed only upon very close examination of the stitch. However, when decorative or specialty threads are used, the need for this adjustment may become glaring. This is again one of the things that will depend on whether or not the person pushing the foot control is a perfectionist.

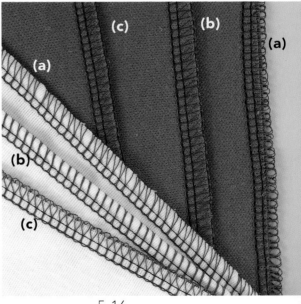

5-16

Tension Disk Cleaning and Maintenance

Sometimes careful threading, balancing, and testing does not solve a tension problem. The culprit may be dirt, lint, and dust. The tolerance between the tension disks is sensitive and the disks must touch all the way around. If anything foreign is in the way, it keeps them from doing their job.

The disks need to be cleaned and maintained for maximum quality operating life. Start first by adjusting the tensions to their lowest settings, or release the tensions by raising the presser foot. Then select one of the following methods for cleaning:

◄ **Canned Air** - Some controversy surrounds the use of canned air products. One concern is environmental, though most products available today have been modified to be atmospherically friendly. The other is due to its incorrect use. The air should be used as directed, so be sure to check the label. The nozzle should be aimed 6" - 12" from the part to be cleaned, not on it! Also, be sure to aim so the dust or lint is blown out and away from other parts of the machine. If the air has a mini-straw-like attachment, use it to aim air between the disks. Repeat with all tensions.

5-17

Floss between the disks - Fold a small piece of tightly woven fabric that will not produce its own lint (not corduroy) in half. Place the folded edge between the disks and pull back and forth in a flossing motion. Refold the fabric and repeat with the other tensions. ▶

5-18

Some Odds and Ends on Tension Management

If at 2 a.m., a serger threaded with dark thread has been misbehaving for an extended time, it is either time to go to bed, clean your serging area, or just do something different for awhile! The problem and solution will reveal itself instantly after a break.

Start with the tensions set in the highlighted or centered area — it's a safe place to start and the settings will probably be close. If the machine offers suggested settings on an LED screen or has automatic tension, use them. Adjustments will be slight if any. Adjust the tensions one at a time. If the first adjustment does not solve the problem, return it to where it was and proceed to the next.

Keep a record of settings used for frequently used stitch formations, thread, and fabric. Save research time when the same technique is repeated.

Make small adjustments. For 3- and 4-thread stitch formations, adjust no more than one setting at a time. For a 2-thread configuration, even a half setting will make considerable difference.

The most important tip – DON'T WORRY ABOUT IT. A good machine will hold proper tension and find its own way if it's adjusted to the closest setting. Don't spend hours seeking a flawless, perfect stitch. The sewing machine is used for perfection. You can always evoke the "THREE-FOOT RULE" – if you cannot see it from three feet away, don't worry about it!

a	b	c

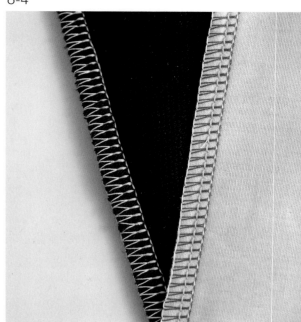

The weight of the fabric determines the cutting width setting. For example, a heavy plush velour needs little fabric under the loops. If there is too much fabric, the seam is bulky and won't lie flat. The cutting width is set low (0 - 1) to have a minimum of fabric in the stitch. In contrast, a lightweight cotton can have more fabric under the loops, so a higher (1.5 - 2) number cutting width is used. Too little fabric encased in the stitch will weaken the seam; too much and it will not lie flat. These are guidelines for settings, not definitive numbers. Understanding the concept will provide guidance, but testing is the only way to be sure. ▶

Extreme changes in the cutting width mean tension changes. The reasons are the same as for stitch length — more or less thread is needed to make a satisfactory stitch. If the cutting width is set at a low number, there is less fabric under the stitch so less thread is needed to cover the fabric. Less thread means tightening (higher number or "+") the tension. A larger cutting width, a wider stitch, means more thread. More thread means loosening (lower number or "-") the tension. Again, by testing you will find the perfect stitch.

Differential Feed

Differential feed was once an optional feature on a serger, but not any more! It is a necessary feature and the more you use it, the more uses you will find for it. Differential feed, the ability to change the motion of the feed dogs, was originally touted to be the remedy for the stretching and waving that occurs while serging interlock knits. It certainly does solve that problem, but it can be used for so much more.

INVESTIGATNG
SERGER
CONTROLS

6-5

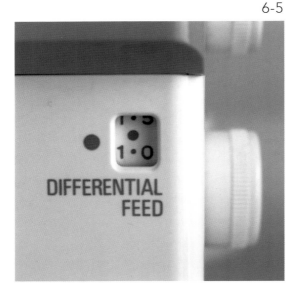

6-6

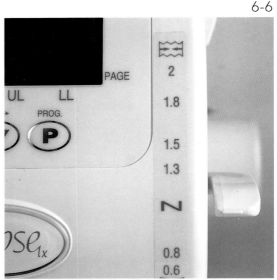

▲ Check your instruction manual for the location and operation of the differential feed control. A control that is located on the exterior of the machine in an easy-to-reach place is preferred because adjustments can be made easily without having to remove the fabric.

6-7

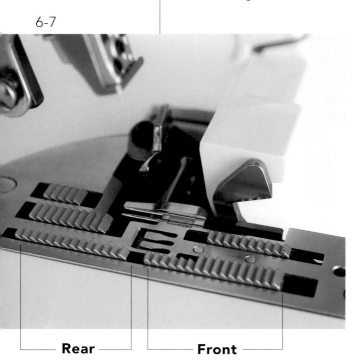

Rear ——— Front ———

◄ A machine with differential feed has two sets of feed dogs: a front and rear set. The front set pushes the fabric to the needle; the back set pulls it from the needle and pushes it out under the foot. The feed dogs operate independently of each other. When set at the neutral or 1 setting, the feed dogs move at the same speed. When the control is set for "+", or more than 1, the front set of feed dogs moves faster than the rear set. For example, when the differential is set at 2, the front set of feed dogs is forcing twice as much fabric under the needle as the rear set is pulling out, automatically easing the fabric. When set for a "-", or less than 1 setting, the front set of feed dogs slightly stretch the fabric before it goes under the needle.

When do you use which setting, and how do you know how much to adjust? Unfortunately, there are no firm or absolute rules, just guidelines. As each fabric and serger behaves differently, only testing will reveal the correct differential setting.

The "+" setting (greater than 1) is used to prevent ▶ stretching, waving, or distortion on knits, ribbing, loosely woven or bias-cut fabrics (a), or on areas that stretch just because! The differential feed pushes or eases extra fabric to the needle. The fabric will not be allowed to stretch (b). Use it to ease straight seams to prevent unsightly waving or on a curved hem or tablecloth that has bias areas.

Practical uses include adjusting the differential instead ▶ of basting rows of straight stitches when putting in a sleeve or when attaching ribbing or a waistband. Because the fabric most affected by the differential feed is the bottom layer, the one next to the feed dogs, the differential feed can also be used to match a pattern or plaid. A "+" setting used on a fabric not likely to stretch results in wonderful, full, even gathers. Adjust the differential feed to the highest setting and use the longest stitch length for soft full ruffles.

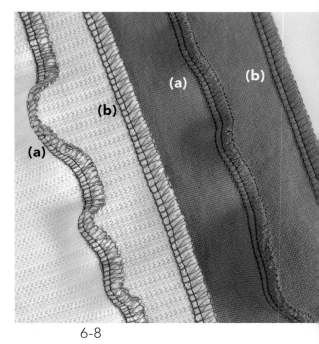

6-8

6-9

6-10

◄ The "+" setting, or less than 1, is used to hold back or stretch the fabric such as lightweight fabrics that may pucker when serged. This puckering is more obvious when using a single layer of fabric, so the differential is used frequently when serging a rolled hem.

Presser Foot Pressure Control

An adjustment to the pressure control affects the movement or feed of the fabric. Correct adjustment means the fabric will feed evenly and smoothly under the presser foot. The fabric is pushed against the feed dogs as it travels through the machine. In most cases, the preset factory adjustment, how the machine comes out of the box, is correct. Adjusting the differential feed may be an easier way to solve feeding problems as it allows finer tuning and is, in many cases, easier to return to normal.

Some sergers don't have an adjustable presser foot pressure control. In that case, baste the fabrics together on the sewing machine before serging. However, some fabrics will need a pressure adjustment. Knits, very fine or slippery fabrics, heavy fabrics, fabrics with a great deal of nap, or fabrics with embroidery, paint, or glitter incorporated in their weave feed more evenly with a pressure adjustment.

When serging knits, rippling or waving denotes a need for pressure adjustment. If differential feed is available, adjust this control to the "+" position. Otherwise, reduce the pressure on the presser foot since symptoms indicate there is too much pressure pushing the foot down on the fabric, holding it back, and stretching it.

Very fine fabrics take up less space between the presser foot and feed dogs, so they may need more pressure to hold them firmly against the feed dogs. Otherwise, the fabric will slip out from under the foot or the layers shift away from each other.

Thick or heavily napped fabrics need less pressure so there is more room under the foot for the bulk and two layers feed together. The same would be true for fabrics with an uneven surface due to embroidery or embellishment.

Changing the pressure varies with the make and model of overlock machine. Some machines have a slide switch with high, medium, and low settings. Others have a large finger screw that is tightened by turning clockwise. This screw isn't marked, so use a marker to indicate the original position for reference. Again, in most cases, the factory adjustment is correct, so don't adjust unless absolutely necessary. ▼

6-11

6-12

CERTIFICATE OF ACHIEVEMENT

TO

FOR MASTERING

BASIC SERGER TECHNIQUES

MASTERING SERGER TECHNIQUES

When using the serger, it's necessary to forget, or relearn, many techniques you've always used on your sewing machine. The serger and the sewing machine are different structurally and mechanically, therefore using them is different. We draw from what we know, but adapt, so we use our time and our tools most efficiently.

The Presser Foot

In Chapter 4, the pros and mainly cons of raising and lowering the presser foot were discussed. If the presser foot is raised and lowered at the beginning and end of each serger seam, there is a possibility that the thread tail will shift and become tangled in the loopers when serging resumes. Plus, that process takes too much time!

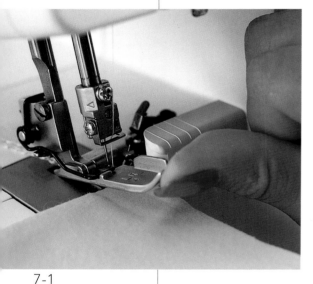

7-1

◄ When serging many layers of slippery or heavy fabric, the only way to get the fabric under the foot is to lift it. But, instead of reaching for the presser foot lifter, the foot can be lifted using the thumb of your right hand. The back of the presser foot holds the thread chain in place but there is now space to push the fabric underneath. Elevating just the front of the presser foot maintains an element of safety, too. The operator's hands and fingers are kept away from the needles and knives. Although it would be difficult to be cut with the serger knives because fingers would need to get in between them, it's not impossible.

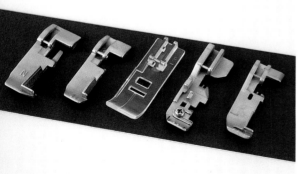

7-2

◄ The presser foot on many machines has markings that are helpful guides. Most feet have dots, lines, or bumps that indicate the approximate location of the right and left needles. Toward the right front edge of the foot is also an indication of the blade position. It may be a cutout, ridge, or small blade-like protrusion. Rather than being overly concerned about the exact measurements and distance from the cut edge, use these markings as your guiding reference.

Serger Seams - Guiding the Fabric

Throughout our sewing lives, to ensure sewing straight seams on the sewing machine, we have been taught to guide the edges of the fabric along the lines on the throat plate. To guide the fabric straight, we watch the raw edges and the line, not the needle.

7-3

Guiding the fabric is different on the serger. First, there ▶ are no lines on the throat plate; actually there is no throat plate — it is a needle plate and does not extend to the right side of the needle. There may be markings to follow, like those on the sewing machine or on the knife cover or front looper cover. If not, there are stick-on tapes available showing seam measurements for easy reference. These marks show where to guide the edge of the fabric so the needle penetration is on the same seam line as if sewn on the sewing machine.

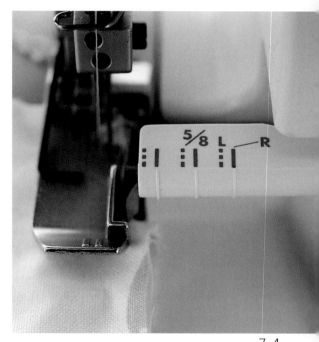

7-4

When using a serger, it's sometimes necessary to watch the needle, or the mark on the presser foot indicating the needle position. This will be the seam line. The intended finished seam line must be lined up with the needle. So, when a garment is designed for a 5/8" seam, approximately 1/4" of fabric should extend beyond the edge of the machine and be cut off. The resulting seam is approximately 3/8" wide, but the finished seam line is 5/8" from the original edge. If the pattern allows for a 1/4"- seam allowance, the fabric should be lined up about even with the blade, and only threads shaved off.

The easiest way to guide the fabric while serging is not to! Let the serger do the work. A very light hand is needed — the serger feed dogs will do the work. You need to gently guide the fabric to regulate how much is cut off, but **never**, **never** pull on the fabric, either in front or in the back of the needle. A looper or needle can bend or worse, break, causing serious mechanical trouble. If you find the amount of fabric being cut varying, slow down, and reposition yourself so you are seated in front, or slightly to the right of the needle. This will give you a more accurate view of where the fabric is feeding.

◄ When serging a seam, first push the fabric under the toe of the presser foot so the feed dogs grab it. Then, place your **left hand**, palm side down, to the left of the presser foot and use just your fingers to guide the fabric. The bed of the machine will support the fabric, unless large heavy pieces are being serged. Be sure the fabric is supported. The weight and bulk of the piece may keep it from feeding properly and distort the serger stitch. Your **right hand** is used to keep the raw edges together in front of the knife.

One of the first sewing habits that must be immediately broken is using pins to hold the fabric layers together. Pins are not as necessary when serging as when sewing because the serger feed dogs and presser foot pressure hold the layers together more securely. If a pin somehow ends up in the serging path, the machine will serge right through it! However it will be the last thing it will serge smoothly. The blade will cut the pin resulting in a nasty nick on the blade, just as if shears tried to cut a pin. In the worst case, sewing over pins could possibly throw the machine out of alignment.

7-5

If serging slippery fabrics, or curved or ▶ more intricate seams, and there's a need to use pins, place the pins parallel to the seam line, 3/4" - 1" from the seam line not the cutting line. Use large-headed pins that can easily be seen and removed. Try small plastic clothespins, paper clips, covered wire clips or even quilt binding clips to hold the layers of fabrics together. These large, more visible clips are easy to remove before they reach the presser foot.

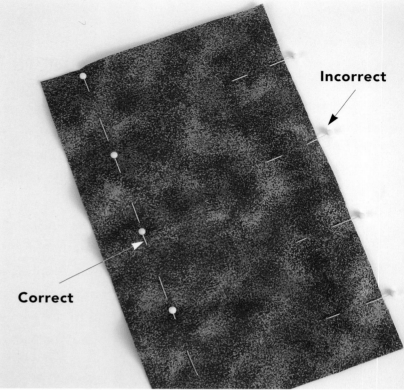

7-6

If pinning is not appropriate, or the fabrics need to be held together more securely, basting is an alternative. Sewing machine or hand basting is sewn just outside the seam line, about 2" from the edge to be trimmed and finished. The basting will be hidden within the serger stitches or can easily be removed.

There are basting tapes available, but they are not suited to all fabrics. The tape is placed between the layers of fabric and carefully positioned so it isn't cut or serged into the seam which makes the needle and blades sticky. Tape works well on sheer fabrics, but with opaque fabrics guiding is a challenge. Some tapes are water soluble for easy removal, but check the fabric first to see if it is washable. For small pieces of fabric use a fabric basting glue or a glue stick. Be sure to use a washable fabric glue, not a paper glue. Match the technique with the fabric, its intended use, and care.

Remember 80% - 90% of the time, just shove (technical serger term!) the fabric under the feed dogs and start serging.

Serger Seams - Securing the Seam

We have serged the perfect serger seam, now we want to be sure it's secure, so we reach for the reverse button. But, it's not there! That's right, a serger goes in one direction – forward. It cannot serge in reverse. But that's not a problem, and another reason why serging is so wonderful – it's fast and easy.

7-7

7-8

The easiest way to secure a serger seam is not to worry about it! Rarely is it necessary to secure the stitch, because it's usually serged over with another seam or finished by adding a waistband or hem. If not, because the serger stitch is, in its own way, crocheted, it's not likely to unravel. If the stitch is located in an obvious area, or one that won't be crossed, there are many ways to secure the ends. None of the methods listed here are complicated or difficult, but they may take some time and handwork.

◄ **Fray Check™, No-Fray™, or other seam sealants** are the favorites aids of those who want security at the end of a serger seam. Place a drop of the seam sealant on the end of the thread chain next to the fabric. Let the threads dry and then cut off the extra chain. Be sure to let the seam sealant dry completely, otherwise it will not fuse the threads.

◄ Another option is to **tie the thread chain in a knot**. First, smooth out the chain so it is long and narrow. Then, tie the threads using a simple overhand knot. Slide and tighten the knot next to the edge of the fabric. Add seam sealant if desired.

7-9

With or without a knot, the ▶ thread chain may be woven back through the serger stitch. Again, smooth out the thread chain. Thread the ends through a large-eye needle, a tapestry needle, a double-eye needle, or a child's small plastic needle, a loop turner, or even a latch hook. If you can find an old knit picker – the crochet-type hook used to fix pulls in double knit fabric years ago – it works well, too. Weave the needle and thread ends back through the serger stitch for 2"- 3". Trim any extra threads and use seam sealant if desired.

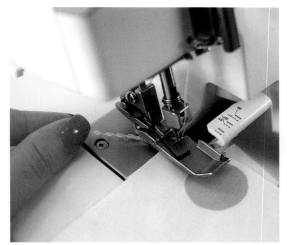

7-10

The strongest, most reliable method for securing the ▶ seam is to oversew the thread tail. Extra steps are needed at the serger, but no handwork. Serge until the overlock stitch is three or four stitches into the fabric (1/4" - 1/2"). Stop, raise the presser foot, and using a needle-down function or the handwheel, lower the needle(s) into the fabric. Smooth out the thread tail.

Bring the thread tail around in front of the needle and ▶ across under the presser foot. Do not pull on the thread so much that the fabric curls; be sure that the corner and edge of the fabric stay flat. Lower the foot and serge over the thread tail, cutting off any extra threads.

7-11

MASTERING
SERGER
TECHNIQUES

7-12

◄ It will take a few practice passes to know how much to pull the thread chain so you don't have a loop or curled edge. This seam finish is visible and attractive. However, it can only be done at the beginning of a seam.

7-13

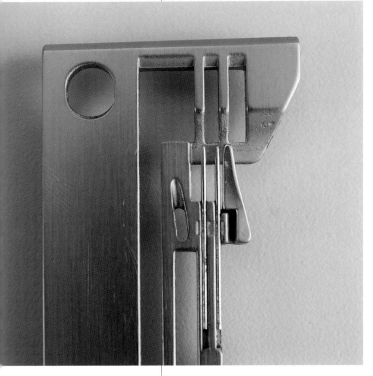

◄ To secure the end of your serging involves clearing the stitch finger. The stitch finger is the piece under the presser foot over which the stitch is formed. It supports the stitch, so for a rolled hem, it is a tiny, narrow rod; for the overlock stitch, it is a flat, 3 - 5 mm piece. You can clear the stitch finger on some machines with a slight "tug" on the fabric, other machines need some extra help.

If the machine adjusts to a built-in rolled hem with a slide switch or knob, it may be possible to move to this position. The needle thread is loosened and a slight pull will clear the stitching from the stitch finger. Remember to return the stitch finger to the regular setting before continuing to serge.

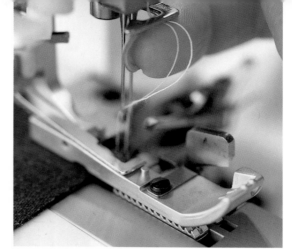

If the fabric will not release, pull slightly on the needle thread(s) just above the needle eye to create some slack. Then, a gentle tug should release the fabric. ▶

7-14

To secure the ends of a serger seam, serge three to four stitches off the end of the seam. Raise the needle(s) to its highest position, then raise the presser foot. Clear the stitch finger using one of the above suggested methods. Flip the fabric over and place it under the foot at a slight angle. Serge, being careful not to cut the previous serging. Serge off the fabric and trim the extra thread tail. ▶

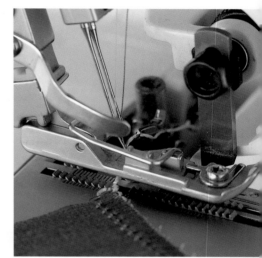

Removing Serger Seams

7-15

Unfortunately, every once in a while, it's necessary to "reverse serge" or rip out a serged seam. The easiest way is to trim off with either the serger, a rotary cutter, or scissors. Sometimes, however, trimming isn't possible and it's necessary to remove the stitching, thread by thread.

When using a 3- or 4-thread overlock stitch, first serge ▶ off the fabric, creating a thread tail approximately 6" long. Smooth out the thread tail at the end of the seam. There are two long threads and one or two short threads. The short one(s) are the needle threads; the longer ones are the looper threads. This makes sense as it takes more thread to form the loops than stitch through the fabric.

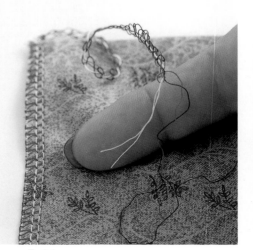

7-16

7-17

7-18

▲ Pull the needle thread(s), sliding the fabric over the thread(s). The fabric will gather, but keep pulling. Eventually the needle thread will be entirely removed. The looper threads will now pull away in a long continuous thread, because the needle thread is no longer holding them in place. If the needle thread breaks while you are pulling, repeat the process from the other end of the seam, or separate the threads to reveal the needle thread(s) again. This method works for many fabrics and stitch formations, but some fabrics will not slide on the thread or themselves, or a fine thread will keep breaking. So, other methods for removing seams are available.

7-19

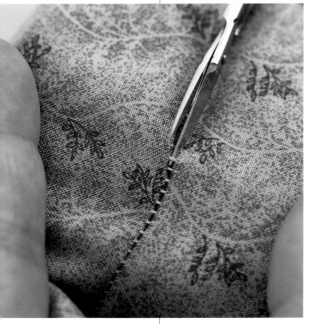

◄ Using the traditional sewing method of removing seams is an option in some situations. Pull the seam open and pick out the needle thread using a seam ripper or small embroidery scissors. This method can be very time consuming, especially if two needles were used.

7-20

A type of seam ripper called a surgical seam ripper is ▶ ideal for the next technique. Simply run the seam ripper between the two layers of fabric enclosed in the serger seam. This ripper will cut the upper and/or the lower looper thread. Then, the needle thread can easily be removed and looper threads picked out.

An alternative to this method would be to cut only one looper thread, releasing the other looper and loosening the needle thread for easier removal. The exasperating part of using these two methods is the resulting small bits of thread that need to be picked off the fabric. When as many threads as possible are shaken off, try a piece of wide masking tape or a lint removal brush or roller to remove the rest.

Serging Corners

Serging corners for edge finishing or in construction can save a tremendous amount of time. In a few cases, a small amount of accuracy may be lost, but remember, if accuracy is absolutely essential, use the sewing machine! In fact, the easiest way to serge an angled corner is to turn it into a rounded one. It often won't make a difference.

MASTERING
SERGER
TECHNIQUES

7-21

Outside Corners

Outside corners are those found on napkins, scarves, cuffs, and collars. Test to determine the best procedure to use for the location, fabric, and stitch formation selected.

▲ **The Serge-Off and Turn Corner:** Simply, serge off the fabric, rotate the fabric 90° and while using the thread tail to guide the fabric back into the machine, cut off the thread tail, and continue serging. The narrower the stitch formation, the better this technique looks (for example, a rolled hem looks better than the wide 4-thread stitch). Some fabrics may stretch slightly when using this method.

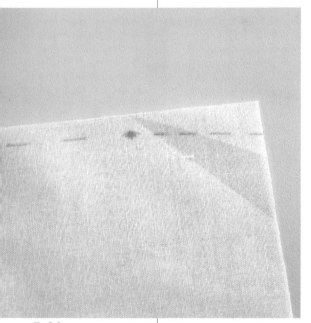

7-22

◄ Use the following technique to avoid distorted corners. With a fabric marker, place a dot about 2" from the corner. Serge to the dot. Continue serging, cutting off slightly more fabric, but not more than an additional 1/8" all the way to the end. Rotate the fabric 90°. Serge back onto the fabric either a) by angling out, cutting off slightly less fabric, or b) by using the thread tail to guide the corner back into the machine. A slight pull on the thread tail will reshape the corner into the desired angle. Use seam sealant and clip the thread tail.

The Knife Window: This method works well with a wider stitch formation, when continuous serging, and no thread tails to finish and trim is desired. It may take a few practice tries to perfect, but this method is worth it. ▶

To make this method work, trim 1/4" or more off the second edge of the corner. Trim this edge, 3" x 1/4" for the knife.

7-23

Serge the first side until the needle is one or two stitches off the fabric. Turn the handwheel or use the needle up/down button, if available, to raise the needle to its highest position. Clear the stitch finger. Be sure there is no extra slack in the needle thread or there will be unwanted loops of thread at the corner. Rotate the fabric and position it so the knife is next to the trimmed edge and the needle is just off the top edge of the fabric. Continue serging. For greater precision, take the first stitch by turning the handwheel so the needle is in the fabric. Prepare the next edge in the same manner and continue serging. For a napkin or scarf, three sides are trimmed and the fourth is finished by just serging off the edge. ▶

7-24

The Wrapped Corner or Edge: Use this method for construction when the seam will be between layers of fabric, such as, on a collar. You may think this method adds extra bulk in the corner or at the angle, but this isn't the case.

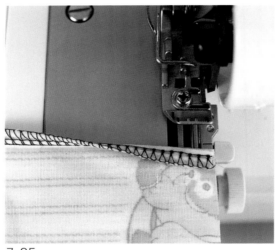

7-25

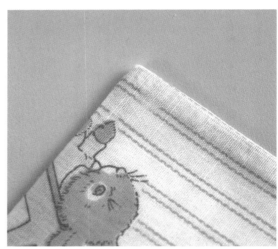

7-26

▲ Set the serger for a 3- or 4-thread stitch. Place the right sides of the fabric together and serge the longest edge first. For a square, serge two parallel sides first, then repeat with the other sides. Serge off the edge. Press the seam flat, then fold the edge back and press the seam toward the body of the fabric. Serge, being sure the folded and pressed seam stays toward the fabric. Press again and turn the piece right side out. There is no need to trim or clip any corners. The result will be a perfect angle.

Inside Corners

Inside corners are a bit more challenging than outside corners. There are fortunately fewer inside corners in construction and most can be rounded without altering a design. Again, if accuracy and precision are imperative, use the sewing machine. An inside corner may be a slit in a skirt, a sleeve placket, a square neckline seam or finish, or an edge finish.

The technique to serge ▶
an inside corner is, simply,
to pull the inside corner
into a vertical line while
stitching. This technique is
easiest when a minimum,
just a few threads, of fabric

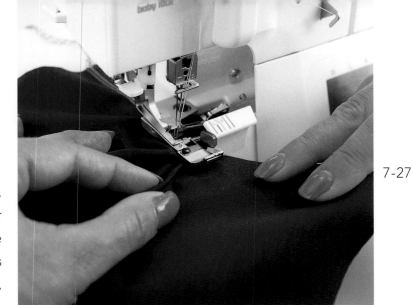

7-27

is cut away. If it is essential to remove the 5/8" seam allowance, trim
off 1/2" before serging. Lines or tucks may form at the corner point.
If so, serge slowly, using finger tips to ease the fabric at the corner.
These tucks will disappear when the fabric returns to the angle.

Serging Curves

Serging a curved seam is a simple operation as long as the curve ▶
is not too sharp. The serger will do an accurate job on a curve only
so far because the blade and needle are far apart from each other
and the presser foot is long. There is very little space for maneuver-
ing around a curve.

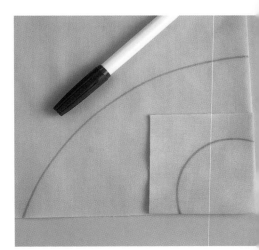

7-28

If an outer edge is curved, to keep the curve accurate ▶
and even, serge for a very short distance, raise the presser
foot, pivot the fabric, and repeat. It's necessary to lift the
foot more frequently than on the sewing machine because
it's longer and holds the fabric in place more securely. Plan
your serging so there is seam allowance to trim since the
serger stitch always looks better when some fabric is
trimmed away, even just a few threads. Trimming also
assures the same amount of fabric under the loops.

7-29

7-30

Serging in a Circle

▲ Serging circles has the same limitations as serging curves; if the circle is too small, it's impossible to be completely accurate and even. There are different methods for circles depending on whether the edge of the circle will be trimmed, how visible it will be, and operator skill.

If the edge isn't to be trimmed or is just slightly shaved, follow these steps: Begin serging, by angling the stitches onto the fabric. **Note:** If this serging is a visible edge finish, cut a knife window as explained in Serging Corners, page 101, and start serging in that area. If the item is oval, start and finish along the straightest edge.

Serge around the circle, trimming away a very small amount. After completing the circle, continue serging, overlapping the stitch 1/2" - 3/4". While overlapping stitches, you can move the blade out of the way so the original stitches are not cut, or guide the fabric very slightly to the left. When the serging is complete, raise the presser foot and clear the stitch finger. Continue serging creating a 4" - 6" thread tail. Stop serging. Use seam sealant and clip the tail or pull the thread tail back through the serger stitch.

Using the Serger to Hem

In this section, hemming does not mean rolled hemming. Hemming in this case means using the 3- or 4-thread overlock stitch to hem. The rolled hem will be discussed in a future chapter. This method also does not include using a blind hem foot, a readily available accessory foot for the serger.

There are a number of ways to approach hems using the overlock stitch. The stitch chosen will depend on the use, fabric, thread, and care of the project.

7-31

The easiest way to hem using the serger is not to hem in ▶ a conventional sense, at all! Use the overlock stitch to finish the single edge and leave it at that. If a sleeve, for instance, will be rolled up, this is perfect - a finished edge with no additional bulk. Decorative thread could be used for a more obvious edge. If the fabric is very fine or loosely woven, turn under 1/4" - 3/8" and serge over this fold. The edge will have a bit more weight and the fabric will be finished twice, with a fold and overlock stitch.

The next method is to use the serger to finish the raw ▶ edge and then turn up an actual hem. This hem could be completed using a sewing machine blind hem stitch, topstitched with single or double needles, or, if absolutely necessary, by hand! Some fusible products can eliminate some steps from this process. Fuse the hem in place using strips of fusible web between the hem and the garment, or use fusible thread in the lower looper. When the hem is turned up and pressed, the tape or thread holds it in place. For some projects, this fusing may be the final step; others may need topstitching or the hem finished in a more traditional manner.

7-32

UNRAVELING KNIT NONSENSE

When sergers were first introduced to the home sewing market, they were defined as the machine to use when sewing knit fabric. We know the serger is capable of much more than that but we still recognize just how fabulous a serger is when using knit fabrics. Pattern companies are finally including serger directions in what they consider to be appropriate patterns. Those who create their own fashions want more. This chapter will not be project specific, but offer techniques and information to adapt to any fabric that stretches.

UNRAVELING
KNIT
NONSENSE

8-1

The Many Faces of Knit Fabrics

▲ Knits are comfortable to wear, easy to care for, and come in a wide range of colors, fabric types, and weights. They may be lightweight, cotton interlocks or jersey; middle-weight double knit blends, sweater knits, or fleece; or heavy-weight stretch terry or velour. They may be brightly colored lycra for active wear, or soft, pastel interlocks for night wear. They can be extra absorbent for comfort during sports activities, or repel moisture, wind, and cold when you're caught outdoors. After deciding what type of knit fabric to use, knit garments are easy to cut, fit, seam, and finish.

When using knit fabrics, the first step is to preshrink the fabric. Treat the fabric as if it is the finished project. Check the end boards when purchasing fabric to see if there are any special washing instructions. You don't want to spend hours sewing a garment that can only be worn once because it was washed or cleaned improperly.

8-2

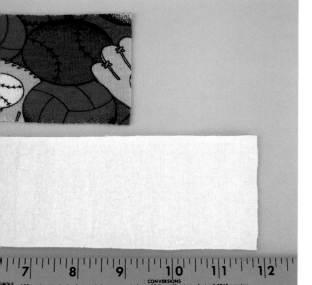

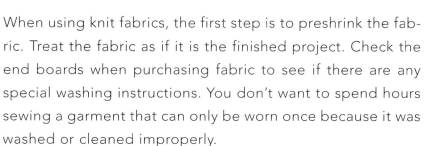

◄ Knit fabric has the outstanding characteristic of stretching. The serger provides a stitch that stretches as much as the fabric being serged. What a perfect combination! The inherent stretch in the fabric may be lengthwise, crosswise, or in the case of lycra, in both directions. It's wise to carefully examine and test the stretch while planning a project so the

Comfort dictates that the seat of shorts or pants, or the area across the shoulders and chest give or stretch while wearing. The fabric should be cut so the most stretch is going around the body. To test the percentage of stretch in a knit fabric, cut an 8" strip across the part of the fabric with the most stretch. If it stretches from:

8" to 10" the stretch is 25%;
8" to 12" the stretch is 50%;
8" to 14" the stretch is 75%; and
8" to 16" the stretch is 100%

The other factor fitting into this equation is "recovery or memory" — whether or not the fabric will return to its original size and shape. A quality knit fabric will recover 80% - 100% while wearing and 100% after washing or cleaning.

Setting Up the Overlock Machine for the Best Results

Correct machine setup in the early stages of your project saves time later. Always start with a clean serger and a new needle. A #70 - #80 universal needle should be appropriate for most weights of knit fabric, but occasionally, a ballpoint needle is needed. Skipped or incomplete stitches mean that something is wrong with the needle and needs to be changed more frequently than for woven fabric serging. A dull needle will break and weaken fibers resulting in small holes along the seam line. Listen for a punching or popping sound as the needle goes through the fabric; also pull the seam open to check for needle damage.

UNRAVELING
KNIT
NONSENSE

8-3

▲ For knit garment construction, set the serger for a 3- or 4-thread balanced overlock stitch. Technically a 3-thread stitch has more stretch than a 4-thread, but for most fabrics the difference is slight.

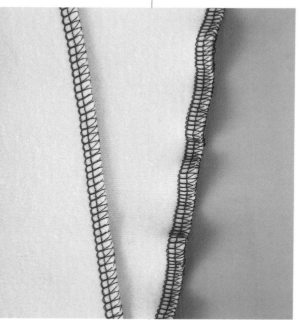

8-4

All-purpose polyester or cotton/polyester thread is suitable for most knit fabrics. Adding a silicon lubricant on the thread assists serging on some specialty knits. It decreases the friction on the thread going through a densely knitted fabric. Another wonderful thread is textured nylon thread. It can be used in the needles and/or in the loopers. This thread stretches, making it a perfect partner for knit fabrics and the serger.

◄ The stretch in the fabric offers the biggest serging challenge. When knit fabrics are sewn on a sewing machine, seams often wave because the fabric stretches while being sewn. They stretch even more when serged due to the increased speed and larger feed dogs. To prevent this from happening, use the differential feed. Test to determine how much differential feed is needed.

Serging ribbing around the bottom of a shirt or top can be challenging. The challenge comes when the ribbing and garment are quartered and matched and there is LOTS of extra garment fabric. The differential feed is very important as it eases in the extra fabric, while the ribbing is stretched, but not so much that it is unable to recover. Be sure to serge with the garment on the bottom, next to the feed dogs.

Hemming Knit Fabrics

Knit garment hems are more professional-looking if they are no more than an 1" - 1 1/2" deep. With more traditional hems, the serger is used to finish the edge of the fabric, then the hem is turned up and held in place in some other manner.

Some of the newer model sergers have a cover stitch, ▶ also called the cover hem stitch. With this stitch, the hem is turned under, and from the right side, the fabric edge is finished and garment hemmed at the same time. If this stitch formation is not available on your machine, you have other choices.

8-12

When finishing a hem edge, serging is done across ▶ the stretch of the fabric, perhaps creating unwanted waves and distortion. The simplest way to remedy this problem is to use the differential feed, but additional stabilization can be added. Place a narrow ribbon or twill tape into the taping guide while serging, being careful not to pull on the ribbon or tape or it will gather the edge. Some edges may need only the addition of a heavy thread such as pearl cotton encased in the serger stitch. If the turned-and-stitched hem needs to stretch (children's pant legs, tightly fitted tops), use elastic cord or narrow clear elastic.

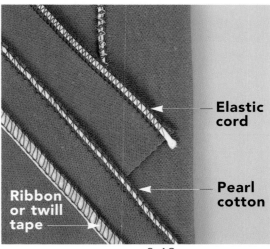

Elastic cord

Pearl cotton

Ribbon or twill tape

8-13

115

UNRAVELING
KNIT
NONSENSE

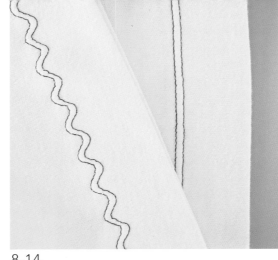

8-14

8-15

◄ A more durable hem is the finish and turned hem. Serge the hem edge, engaging differential feed if necessary. Turn the hem up and finish with a sewing machine blindhem, a zigzag, or a straight-stitch topstitch, or turn up the fabric twice and topstitch. To create a cover stitch look-alike, repeat the above steps, then, from the right side, stitch with a double needle. The zigzag that results on the wrong side of the hem will allow some stretch, ideal for knits.

◄ A quick traditional-looking hem is done using fusible thread in the lower looper. For best results when using fusible thread, use a wide stitch width and a stitch length of 2.5mm - 3mm allowing the maximum amount of fusible thread to be exposed. Serge with the right side of the fabric up. Turn the hem up and fuse in place. The fused hem may not hold through numerous washings. Try it as a basting method and complete with a blindhem, topstitching, or double needle on the sewing machine.

Inside
thread

A Primer on Elastic

Braided Elastic (a) - This polyester elastic is used in casings for waistbands and cuffs, but can be serged directly to the garment. It has a lengthwise parallel network of fibers that narrow when it is stretched. It is sold in widths from 1/8" - 1" wide. The wider widths have more stretch and better recovery.

Knitted Elastic (b) - Polyester, knitted elastic is softer than braided elastic and ideal for direct serger application. It is comfortable worn next to the skin and retains its shape when stretched. A strong, but soft elastic, it is best used on light- to medium-weight fabrics.

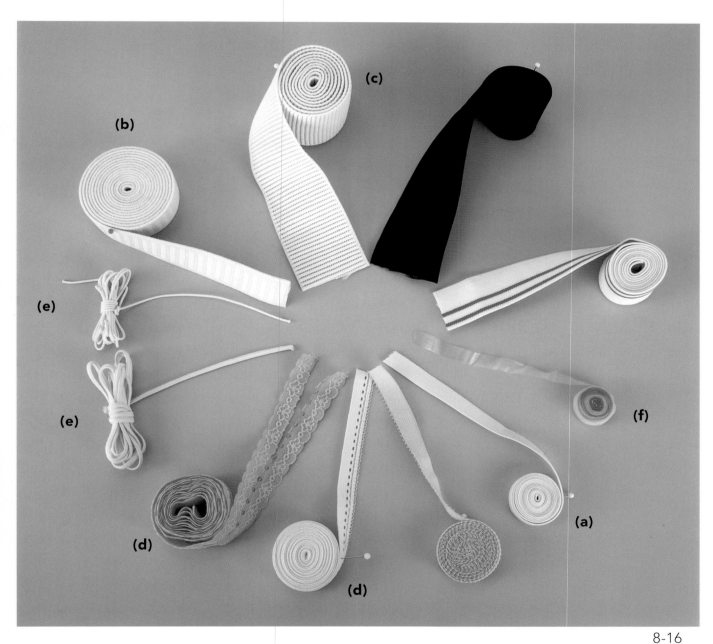

8-16

Non-Roll Woven Elastics (c) - Non-roll elastic is best used in a casing, though it can be serged on one edge. The heavy lateral rib weave keeps it from rolling or twisting, particularly in waistbands. It is available in 3/4" - 2" widths and is recommended for heavier fabrics.

Lingerie Elastic (d) - Lingerie elastic may be made from polyester, cotton, or a blend, and is a braided elastic. It is soft, strong and sometimes has one straight edge and one picot edge. The straight edge can be serged directly to the garment. The addition of cotton creates an absorbent, breathable elastic.

Oval or Round Cord Elastics, Elastic Threads (e) - Polyester elastic cord is used to strengthen and stabilize a serged edge. It is attached using a narrow overlock stitch, which acts as a thread casing. The cords are thin, 1/16" to 1/8" round. Nylon elastic thread is slightly heavier than regular thread and can be used in the loopers to shirr fabric.

Clear Elastic (f) - While clear elastic is relatively new to the home sewing market, it's been used commercially in bathing suits and baby clothes for many years. It's made of polyurethane, is lightweight and thin, but very strong. Heat sensitive, it will melt if touched with direct heat, but is chlorine resistant and repels oils. It is not weakened by continuous needle holes, and will not easily nick lengthwise with the serger blade. Clear elastic must be applied directly, or it will roll. Widths available are 1/4" - 1".

Applications - Casings or Direct?

When serging, elastic is incorporated into a project either by direct application or by forming a casing and threading the elastic through it.

When using a direct application method, choose a 3- or 4-thread overlock stitch. Other stitch options include a flatlock or the cover stitch. Increase the stitch length to 3mm - 3.5mm. Too much thread in and on the elastic inhibits its recovery. A longer stitch length means fewer needle holes to split or damage elastic fibers.

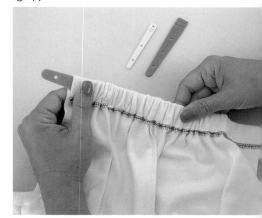

8-17

The waistline casing used frequently in commercial patterns is created by serge-finishing the top of the waistline, then turning down the fabric, 1 1/4" - 1 1/2" to the wrong side. The serged edge is topstitched in place and elastic threaded through the casing. This is a tried-and-true method and best when not sure of the elastic fit. ▶

8-18

A fast casing can be created in one serger step. Leave the center back or a side seam open. Fold the allotted waistband over (usually 1 1/4") then turn the fabric back again as if doing a sewing machine blindhem. Serge through the fold and the fabric edge. Thread the elastic through the waistband casing, then finish the opening with the serger or the sewing machine. It will appear as if a separate waistband casing piece has been added. This technique will take a very small bit of length away from the waist to crotch lengths, so plan ahead for any potential fitting problem by adding 1/4" - 1/2" when cutting out the pattern. ▶

Lycra

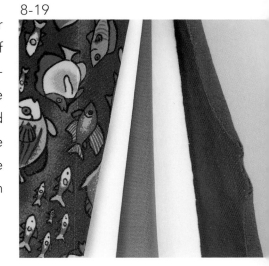

8-19

Lycra fabric conjures up visions of tight-fitting bicycle pants or dancing or skating costumes in vibrant colors. The stretch quality of this fabric is often 90% - 100%. Glossy, high-sheen lycra fabric, usually 20% lycra and 80% nylon, is durable and dries very quickly. The duller, matte-finish lycra is a cotton/lycra mix, absorbent when used for leotards or tights, but takes longer to dry. Test not only for the stretch, but for the recovery when choosing this fabric type. The garment needs to recover the tight fit after being stretched when wearing. ▶

In most cases, lycra stretches in both the lengthwise and crosswise direction but possibly in different amounts. Plan and cut the pattern so the most stretch is going around the body. It may mean cutting pattern pieces in an out of the ordinary way.

A wide 3- or 4-thread overlock stitch or a 3-thread super stretch stitch available on some model overlock machines should be used for the construction of lycra garments. These stitch formations will offer maximum stretch and a wide stitch width means greater durability.

A new #70 or #80 universal needle is essential. The needle will probably need to be changed more frequently due to the abrasion of the synthetic fiber and the density of the fabric. Skipped stitches are a frequent problem with lycra.

8-20

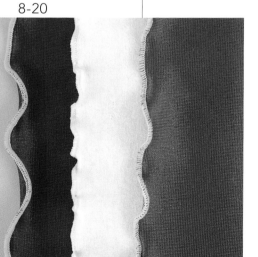

Woolly Nylon™ thread, in the looper and needles, is a good choice for a lycra garment as it's soft and comfortable next to the skin. Most important, though, is that it stretches with the fabric, in the lengthwise and crosswise direction. Polyester thread or polyester/cotton threads can also be successfully used.

◄ Because lycra fabrics don't ravel or fray, they don't need to be hemmed, but do look more finished with an edge treatment. Often the edge will have elastic, but if not, an alternative is to use a lettuce-edge finish. Select a rolled hem or a narrow, overlocked edge.

Tricot

Tricot is a favorite fabric for lingerie because it is soft ▶ and comfortable next to the skin, and lightweight enough not to add bulk under clothes. It is a washable, durable fabric, and does not wrinkle. Manufactured in many colors and sold in widths of 72" - 108", its luxurious drape comes from the type of weave and nylon content in the fabric. To find the right side, stretch the piece. The edge will roll to the right side.

8-21

Tricot should be cut so the stretch is going around the body. There is ease in both directions, but only stretch crosswise, so cut accordingly. Due to tricot's slippery nature, support the extra fabric while cutting and serging.

New #70 - #80 universal needles prevent pulls or damage to tricot fibers. The needle needs to be changed more frequently as even a slight ding or burr could mar the fabric.

8-22

Depending on the fabric weight, a narrow, balanced 3-thread overlock stitch, a rolled hem, or a flatlock stitch is suitable for construction. Select a polyester, a polyester/cotton, or Woolly Nylon™ thread for the loopers and the needles. Rayon or cotton embroidery threads can be used for decorative, low-stress areas.

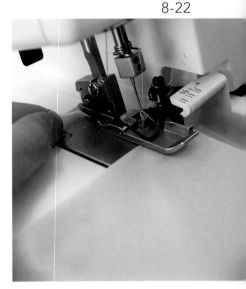

Because tricot is very soft, it may not want to cooperate when feeding under the presser foot. Hold onto the thread chain and guide, not pull, the fabric when starting a seam. This may also be the remedy for a fabric that puckers. ▶

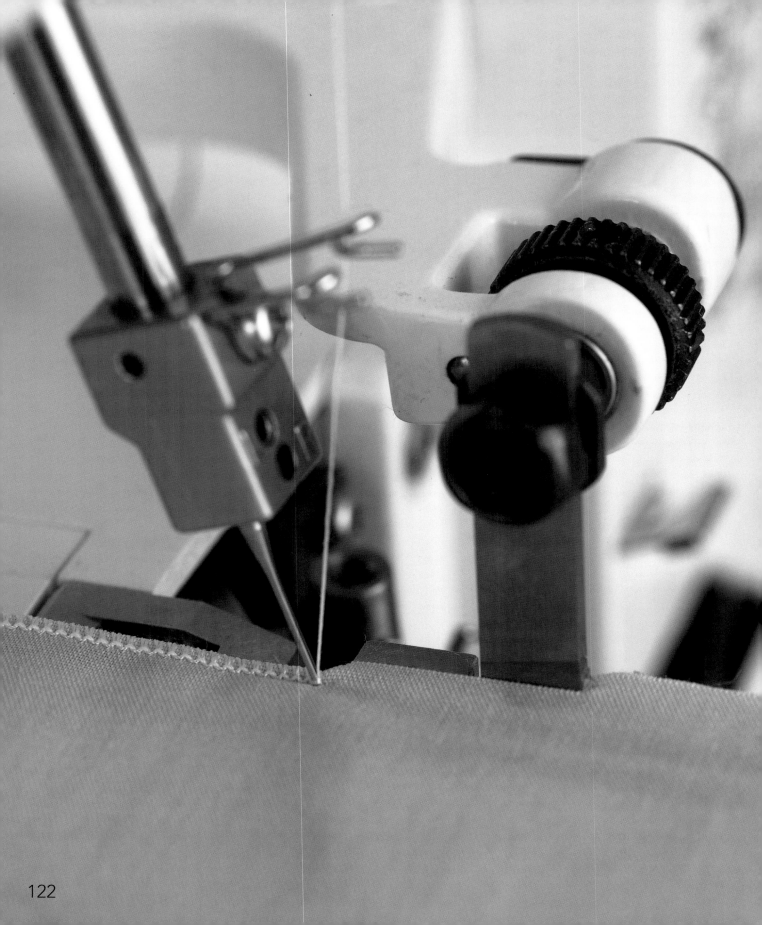

ROLLED HEM RIOT

The narrow rolled edge, more popularly known as the rolled hem, is the beautiful serger finish associated with the edge of napkins and scarves. It appears to be fragile and delicate, but is actually a strong, durable stitch that can be used for an edge finish, a seam, or for interesting decorative details. Until overlock machines were available to the domestic market, duplicating this commercial look was a long, tedious, and not always successful process. Now, a twist of a dial or a movement of a slide results in a quick change to the rolled hem stitch formation.

ROLLED
HEM
RIOT

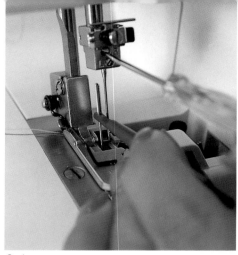

9-1

The Needle

▲ The rolled hem stitch is created with one needle and one or two loopers. For many 3- and 4-thread machines, this means that the left needle must be removed, leaving just the right needle. If the left needle remains in place, the serger will make a wide rather than a narrow stitch and the resulting rolled hem will be ragged and uneven.

9-2

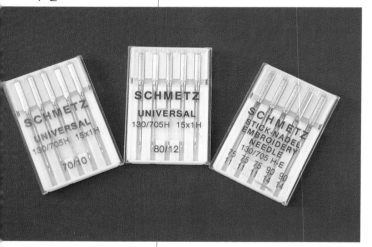

◄ A new, universal needle offers the best results when serging a rolled hem. Fine fabrics such as batiste or silk need a #65 - #70 (size 11 - 12) needle. A #80 (size 14) needle is suitable for other fabrics. If fine rayon, cotton, or metallic thread is used in the needle, an embroidery needle may help to prevent the shredding or breakage that can occur with specialty threads.

Stitch Width

Using the right needle dictates that the rolled hem is a narrow stitch. To further narrow this stitch, a change must be made in the stitch finger, the support over which the stitch is formed. The wider finger used for regular stitching is moved out of the way for roll hemming leaving a slender rod. In some machines, this means the needle plate and, possibly, the presser foot are changed. For machines with a built-in rolled hem, the rolled hem adjustment is made with a lever, dial, or switch that moves the wider part of the stitch finger out of the way.

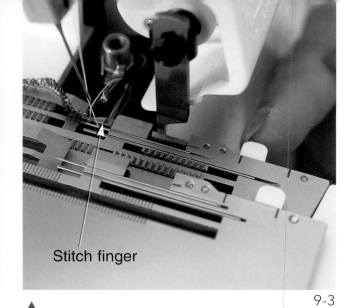

Stitch finger

Stitch finger

▲

9-3

9-4

Now the fabric between the needle and the cut edge of the fabric is wider than the stitch finger. The extra fabric must go somewhere, so it rolls.

The cutting width adjustment also affects the rolled hem stitch width. For rolled hems, this adjustment is used to fine-tune and perfect the stitch by altering the amount of fabric encased in the roll.

9-5

Stitch Length

A rolled hem can be a very short satin stitch (1mm - 1.5mm), but it's more attractive as a slightly longer stitch (1.5mm - 2mm). When the stitches are too close together there's not enough room for the threads to lie flat, so the hem doesn't look smooth and even. If the stitch length is too short, the fabric doesn't feed properly and jams underneath the presser foot. To prevent this, start with a longer stitch and shorten it until the desired look is achieved. ▶

If a satin stitch effect is desired, choose a Woolly Nylon™ thread that will fluff and fill in the space, or use two strands of regular thread for heavier coverage. Heavier decorative threads may be utilized, but they must be soft enough to roll around the fabric.

Rolled Hem Tension Settings

The rolled hem can be stitched with two or three threads. A 3-thread rolled hem is the most commonly used; the 2-thread provides a slightly finer, lighter look. Some fabrics won't roll successfully with a 3-thread stitch but will with a 2-thread, and vice versa. The tension setup is different for each, but the goal for both is a tight, smooth, even roll.

When testing the rolled hem, use the same fabric and threads to be used in the finished product, and, if appropriate, test lengthwise, crosswise, and curved areas. For a better-looking stitch, always cut off some fabric when serging. This ensures a consistent amount of fabric rolled inside the hem. When calculating your finished size, allow 3/8" - 1/2" extra fabric for cutting and rolling.

Serger setup for a 3-thread rolled hem:

9-6

1. Adjust the serger for a balanced 3-thread overlock stitch using the designated rolled hem needle. Your stitch length should be 1.5mm - 2mm; the differential feed set on neutral; and the cutting width set slightly less than normal.

2. Tighten the lower looper ▶ tension, almost as tight as it will go. Test. The upper looper thread should be pulled all the way around to the back, rolling the fabric with it.

3. If the upper looper thread is not pulled to the back, tighten the lower looper more and/or loosen the upper looper tension slightly. Again test.

◀ **4**. If there is any puckering at the seam line, reduce the needle tension slightly, engage the differential feed or hold the fabric taut.

9-7

5. Continue testing until the upper looper thread encases the fabric and the lower looper thread can barely be seen. When properly balanced, the lower looper thread becomes a straight thread on the back side of the fabric. ▶

Note: If the lower looper thread will not tighten enough to pull the upper looper thread around, replace the lower looper thread with textured nylon thread, and lower the tension to the middle range. Test and increase the lower looper tension slightly until the desired result is achieved. Because the textured nylon is very strong and has built-in stretch, it will offer more tension at a lower setting.

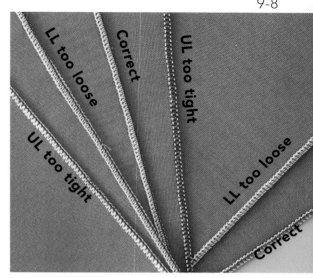
9-8

Serge setup for a 2-thread rolled hem

1. Adjust the serger to a narrow, balanced 2-thread overlock stitch using the stitch length, the differential feed, and cutting width settings as above.

2. Gradually tighten the needle thread and test until ▶ the looper thread is pulled all the way to the back, rolling the fabric. Tighten the tension in small steps as small changes in 2-thread tensions make a big difference in the stitch. If necessary, loosen the looper tension slightly.

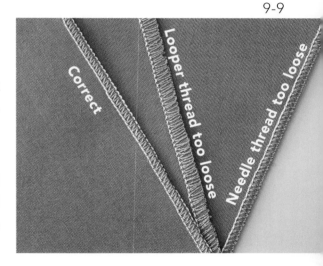
9-9

Notes on Fabric and Threads

The rolled hem is a fabulous finish on numerous types ▶ of fabrics, but not all. There is a point when the fabric is too thick or bulky to roll. A stiff fabric, whether due to its weave, fabric type, or finish, will fight to remain flat and smooth. Sometimes preshrinking softens the fabric and makes it suitable, but if not, another edge finish treatment is necessary. A fabric with a heavy, raised, or flocked-type design

9-10

ROLLED
HEM
RIOT

may not roll consistently. The plain part of the fabric will cooperate, but the design area remains flat. Some techniques for dealing with challenging fabrics will be offered later in this chapter, but sometimes it is necessary to use a narrow overlock stitch as the edge finish, and forget trying to roll hem the fabric.

9-11

◄ The reverse may also be true. A fabric can be too fine or soft to be rolled so a spray starch or a fabric finish is used to give it more body.

All-purpose polyester or poly/cotton thread (c) will make a satisfactory, durable, and boring rolled hem. If you want a visible edge finish, many other threads are more exciting. Choose the thread for the desired look, but also consider the use and care of the final product. For a 3-thread stitch, the upper looper thread will be the most visible. The looper thread shows in a 2-thread rolled hem.

9-12

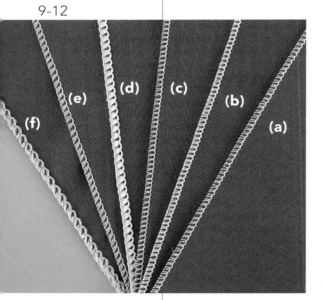

For an elegant classic look, select a fine, lightweight rayon thread (a and b). The sheen of the rayon adds a touch of interest to the edge. The tension on the fine thread is reduced. A heavier rayon thread (d) may be used to make the rolled hem a more obvious part of the design. In bridal sewing, this heavier thread appears like a fine ribbon or crocheted edge on chiffon, organza, or tulle.

◄ Textured nylon, or Woolly Nylon™ thread (e), fluffs and fills in any space between the stitches to provide satin-stitch type coverage. Be sure to loosen the tension on the Woolly Nylon™. For a more interesting look combine Woolly Nylon™ with other threads, or use Double Woolly™ (f).

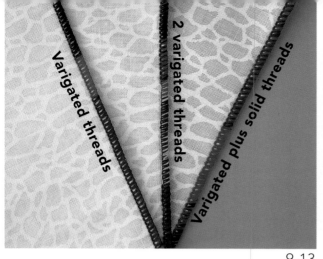

Varigated threads

2 varigated threads

Varigated plus solid threads

9-13

9-14

▲ Variegated threads are attractive in rolled hems. Depending on the type, they often create a brick-like pattern. To vary the look, use two spools of variegated thread in one looper. The variegation in colors still shows, but it's not as distinct. Another option is to mix one of the solid colors in the variegated thread with the variegated one. It softens the variegated look and features one particular color.

Rolled Hem Challenges

Rolled hem challenges appear in many forms. Some are solved with mechanical and setting changes, others need a different combination of fabric or threads. Following are some symptoms and suggested remedies. Try one or a combination in the quest for a perfect rolled hem.

9-15

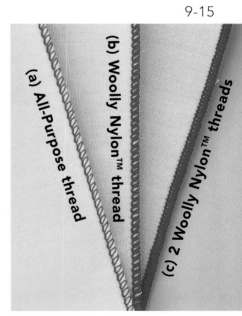

(a) All-Purpose thread

(b) Woolly Nylon™ thread

(c) 2 Woolly Nylon™ threads

Symptom: The fabric won't roll.
• Wash it to remove a stiff finish.
• Tighten lower looper thread (3-thread rolled hem) or needle thread (2-thread) tension to compress the roll of fabric.
• There is a limit; choose another edge finish!

Symptom: The rolled hem stitches do not cover the fabric. ▶
• Alter the design! Rolled hem finishes do not have to be satin stitches. However, if a satin stitch is necessary, or the design calls for a high contrast, investigate these changes.
• Shorten the stitch length. Some tension adjustment may be necessary.

129

ROLLED
HEM
RIOT

9-16

◄ • Multiple strands of thread, as many as four or five strands of light-weight thread, can be used at once. Threads passing through the same tension disk need to be of similar weights. If a desired combination requires very different-weight threads, it is still possible to combine them. For a 3-thread rolled hem, first move the needle thread to the left needle tension disk or slot. Sort the different thread types. Thread one type following the needle thread path until just past the needle tension adjustment, then cross over to the looper tension. Thread the second type like an upper looper thread. Tensions will need to be rebalanced to tolerate all the thread and some wonderful options are revealed.

9-17

• Use Woolly Nylon™ thread in the looper. It will fluff and fill in open areas between stitches. Be sure the tension is loosened.

• Select another edge finish!

◄ **Symptom: The rolled hem puckers.**

• Loosen the needle tension. Set the differential feed to the less than normal or "-" setting. It will now stretch the fabric slightly, having the effect of holding it taut. If differential feed is unavailable, hold the fabric tightly in front of and behind the presser foot while serging.

• Use spray starch or fabric finish to give the fabric a bit more body and stability.

• Select another edge finish!

Symptom: Tiny threads stick out from the rolled hem.

• If the "pokies" face the fabric, there is probably too ▶ much fabric in the roll. Decrease the cutting width, cutting off more fabric.

• If the "pokies" stick out away from the fabric, the problem is that too little fabric is being rolled into the rolled hem. Treat this by increasing the cutting width (adjust to a higher number), cutting off less fabric and leaving more to roll.

• Shorten the stitch length to have more stitches to cover the fabric.

• Loosen the upper looper tension so the thread is not cutting the fabric.

• If the cutting width changes don't make a differ- ▶ ence or a cutting width adjustment is not available, turn the edge of the fabric under 3/8" - 1/2" and press. Serge on the fold. Trim away the extra fabric if it will show in the final use or wearing.

• Select another edge finish.

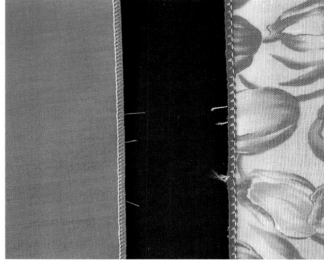

9-18

Symptom: The rolled hem pulls away from the fabric.

This problem occurs when rolled hemming is done with the grain of the fabric and not on the cross grain, or vice versa. Test ahead of time so the cutting of the fabric can be altered if necessary.

9-19

• Increase the stitch length. When using a short stitch length, needle penetrations are very close together and may cut the fabric. A longer stitch length may eliminate this cutting.

• Increase the cutting width to add more fabric to the roll.

ROLLED
HEM
RIOT

• Add more body to the fabric. ▶ Spray starch or finish may be enough or add tricot tape or wash away stabilizer. Fold the fabric under 3/8" - 1/2". Press, then roll hem on the fold.

• Select another edge finish!

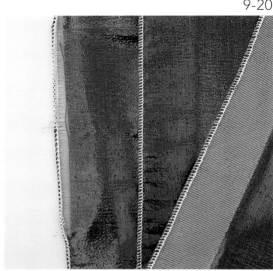

9-21

Uses for the Rolled Hem

◀ The obvious use for a rolled hem, as an edge finish, is where some serger users stop. The rolled hem has many other practical, decorative, and unusual uses.

A rolled hem edge finish can become the major part of the design when corded. The cording may be from pearl cotton and used for reinforcement, or from unusual things like fishing line and floral wire.

9-22

◀ When fishing line is rolled into the hem of a ruffle of a bridal fabric like taffeta or organza, it will give the edge more body and make it stand up for a full, dressy look. Incorporation of floral wire into an edge will make the fabric "pose." When the fabric is bent or formed into a shape, it will stay. This is wonderful for large bows, or other home decorating items. Wire, fishing line, or cording is placed under the normal presser foot and serged into the stitch, or change to a cording foot for easier guiding.

An alternative finish to the traditional rolled hem is the ▶
lettuce edge. Overlock machine setup and thread choices
are the same, but while serging, the edge is stretched.
Stretching can be done manually by pulling the fabric in
front of and behind the presser foot, or by setting the differential feed to a less than normal setting. A combination
of these techniques gets the best results. When stretching
the fabric, be sure to continue serging, so the needle will
not be bent. This works beautifully on knit fabrics, but is
also attractive on many woven fabrics.

Next, the rolled hem thread chain can be used by itself, as
a button loop, belt loop, or decorative chain. Yards of chain
can be wrapped together to make a tassel. Decorative
chain, trims, and braids appear when decorative threads are
used in the loopers or needle. ▶

Lightweight fabrics can be beautifully seamed with the
rolled hem. It provides a fine, even seam with no seam
allowance showing through a sheer fabric. Since this is a
very narrow seam, it's not suited for high-stress areas. A
curved area, such as a collar, would be an excellent place to
use the rolled hem as a seam. If constructed on the sewing
machine, the collar is placed right sides together, sewn,
trimmed, clipped, turned, then pressed. When serged, it is
automatically trimmed, and no clipping is needed because
of the give in the serger stitch. As an alternative, place the
collar pieces, wrong sides together, and serge. There will be
no need to turn the collar, and it will have a piped edge
appearance. ▶

9-23

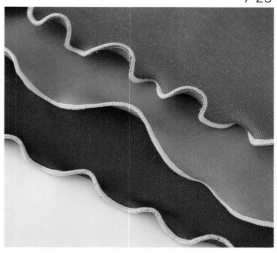

9-24

9-25

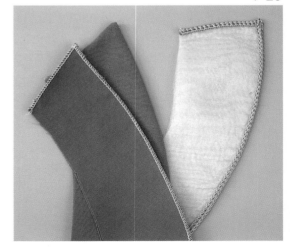

FLATLOCKING— FUNCTIONAL AND FUN

When a new serger owner is first introduced to an overlock machine, the question is often asked, "Is that all it can do?" The answer is "Yes, but..." and the flatlock stitch formation is one of the most popular "buts". A rebalancing of tensions creates a stitch that was developed to imitate a commercial cover stitch. It is flat, fabric edges are butted together or just barely on top of each other, and there are no bumps or lumps from seam allow-ances, making flatlocked garments comfortable to wear.

The flatlock stitch can be used as the main construction stitch, holding seams together, or as decorative work on a fold. Though more durable on fabrics that don't ravel, there are ways to successfully flatlock fabrics of all weights, from edging laces to fake fur.

Flatlocking is a reversible stitch; it has two right sides. Depending on whether the fabrics are serged with right or wrong sides together, a different stitch will show on the top or right side.

10-1

If the fabric is serged with the wrong sides of the fabric together, the "loop" part of the stitch will be displayed. The loop logically is the looper thread. Here is the opportunity to make the stitch a major part of a design. The entire flatlock stitch is exposed, so it is a perfect place to show off decorative threads. A plain garment now becomes a spectacular one.

◄ If the fabric is serged with the right sides together, the "ladder" part of the stitch will show. The ladders are formed by the needle thread. Different thread can be used in the needle to create a light delicate look or a defined tailored appearance.

Flatlocking - Let's Get Technical

There are a number of different types of flatlock stitching. The machine being used, the fabric and final look desired, and the projects end use are the determining factors in choosing a flatlock type. The goal is always the same — to have a smooth even stitch that, when pulled open, lies perfectly flat.

2-Thread Flatlock

A 2-thread flatlock stitch is known as a natural
flatlock; it needs little if any tension adjustment. It
can be wide or narrow, depending on the needle
used, and is formed with a single needle and single
looper thread. For a heavy decorative look, use the
widest stitch and place a decorative thread in the
looper. For a delicate look on fine fabric, place a
fine thread in the needle to create the ladders.

10-2

To create a 2-thread flatlock, the eye of the upper looper needs to
be blocked to form the stitch. On some brands of sergers, an
attachment is added to the looper, while other brands may have a
built-in converter. ▼

10-3

3-Thread Flatlock

By using three threads and careful tension adjustments, a
3-thread flatlock stitch can be achieved. One needle and
the upper and lower loopers are used. If decorative thread
is to be used, it is threaded in the upper looper. Start with
a balanced overlock stitch and make the following tension
adjustments for flatlocking.

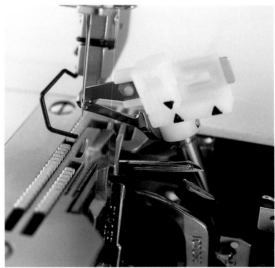

10-4

The tension on the needle thread is reduced to 0 - 1 on a
numerical scale or as far "-" as it will go. In most written
troubleshooting suggestions, they note that when the seam
pulls apart, the needle tension is too loose. This is the ultimate goal: to have the
needle thread tension so loose that it will pull completely apart, allowing the seam
to lie completely flat.

The upper looper thread shows when the loop side is visible. Decorative thread is used here if desired. The tension setting will depend on the thread. Begin by leaving the tension as it is for a balanced stitch. When fine-tuning the stitch, it may be necessary to slightly loosen the tension.

The lower looper thread is tightened to 7 - 9 or as far into the "+" as is possible. It should be tightened so much it pulls the loosened needle thread up to the cut edge of the fabric. So little thread will travel through the lower looper due to the high tension, that the lower looper thread will be a straight line at the cut edge of the fabric. If this looper thread is tightened as far as possible, and it still does not pull the needle thread into position, loosen the upper looper tension slightly.

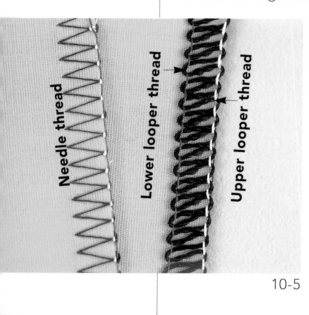

10-5

If additional tension is still needed, thread the lower looper with Woolly Nylon™ thread. Decrease the lower looper tension in half, then gradually tighten it until the desired look is achieved.

◄ When stitching a 2- or 3-thread flatlock, you can determine if your settings are correct even before opening and pulling the stitch flat. After serging, the top side will look like a balanced serger stitch, with loops flat and even between the seam line (needle thread) and the edge of the fabric. The back side has a continuous line of "V"s, formed by the needle thread.

◄ Flatlocking will always be "flatter" if the loops and ladders are the same width. Make careful adjustments when balancing. Don't depend on pressing to flatten the seam. Pressing may even distort and flatten it so much that the final stitch will not be attractive.

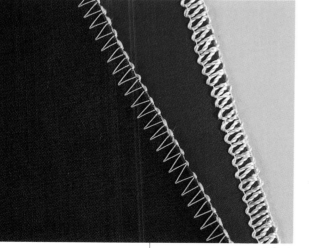

10-6

The 2- and 3-thread flatlock stitches described above are the most recognized types, but there are others that appear in ready-to-wear and can be imitated on the serger. The basic tension theory is explained for each, but it is not a scientific process. Tension adjustments for the desired look vary with type of fabric and threads used.

3-Thread Flatlock with Three Visible Threads

To achieve this stitch formation, some reference guides ▶ instruct you to loosen the needle tension, but leave the upper and lower looper tensions set for a balanced stitch. In reality, loosen the upper looper tension and tighten the lower looper tension until both loops are centered in the stitch. Multiple or different threads can be used to make this stitch formation appear to be a unique trim or braid.

10-7

4-Thread or Safety Stitch Flatlock

This form of flatlocking is done with the overlock ▶ machine threaded for a 4-thread overlock stitch. Both needle thread tensions are loosened and the lower looper tension is tightened until the stitch can be pulled flat. The right needle thread floats in the center of the loop stitches, adding additional interest. The seam will not pull completely flat, though it may appear to. There will be a slight ridge or fold in the center. The ladder part of the stitch will look the same as a 3-thread flatlock.

10-8

FLATLOCKING-
FUNCTIONAL
AND FUN

10-9

Needles and Fabric

▲ To increase the chance for success, always start with a clean machine and new needle. Unless working with lace, batiste, or lingerie-type fabrics that need a #70 - #75 (12) needle, a #80 (14) needle will be the best choice. If fake fur or a fabric with a heavy finish is being serged, a #90 (16) needle may be the best

10-10

choice. However, with the larger needle test carefully, forming the initial stitches by turning the handwheel manually. Listen for any clicking sound that indicates the needle is hitting a looper.

Thread

◄ Almost any thread can be used in a flatlock stitch formation. Evaluate the design and effect desired, and select anything from the finest monofilament thread to the heaviest yarn. Threading of the machine will be the key. If the loops are to be the featured part of the stitch, decorative threads are threaded in the looper. Decorative threads are too costly to be used where no one will see them. To feature the ladders, thread the needle with the decorative thread, selecting the proper needle to accommodate it.

Stitch Width

If the flatlock stitching is going to be decorative or act as the main construction stitch, the widest stitch possible should be selected. If laces and other lightweight fabrics are to be serged, a narrow flatlock will suffice. ▶

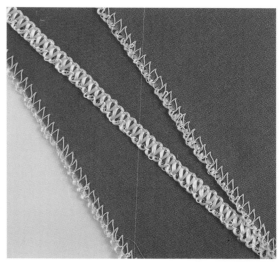

10-11

Stitch Length

The stitch length will be determined by the threads used. Always start with a longer than normal (3mm - 3.5mm) stitch length when using heavier decorative threads. Shorten the length until the desired look is achieved. Starting with too short a length will cause the stitch to jam under the presser foot. Also remember that significant changes in the stitch length may require additional tension adjustment.

Cutting Width

When flatlocking, the cutting width and guiding of the fabric are very closely related. In order for the fabric under the stitches to lie flat, not only must the tension be adjusted correctly, but the correct amount of fabric must also be trimmed away, or with a folded edge, the fold guided correctly under the foot. When seaming fabrics, a lower than normal cutting width is used. For fabrics with texture or bulk, like a sweatshirt fleece, for example, the cutting width is set at its lowest setting, where the largest amount of fabric is trimmed.

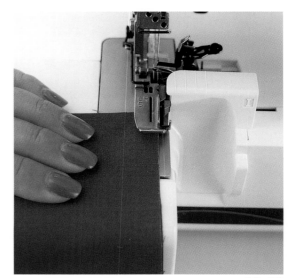

If the flatlocked seam will still not flatten, it may be ▶ necessary to move the edge of the fabric farther to the left. The stitches will actually fall off the edge of the fabric. It will look strange when stitched, but when it is pulled open it will be flat. When flatlocking is done on a fold, the fabric is guided in the same manner, with the edge of the fabric moved to the left so stitches fall off the edge and the fabric is not cut.

10-12

The guiding process will change the finished size of the fabric, if working on a garment, possibly changing the fit and the line. It could add as much as a seam allowance for every seam. Plan and pre-trim your seams if this will be a problem.

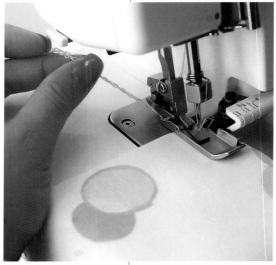

10-13

10-14

It's Time to Serge, but Some Reminders First

1. Try not to raise the presser foot. If more space is needed to position the fabric, lift just the front of the foot.

2. Serge at a smooth even speed, slightly slower than normal. Because of the drastic changes made in tension to achieve this stitch, slow down slightly to let 4"- 6" tail at the start and the end of each seam.

◀ **3**. When using a decorative thread, it is helpful to hold onto the thread chain at the start of the seam, so it doesn't curl around the presser foot and back into the stitch.

◀ **4**. Flatlocked seam intersections need special care. If the thread chain is cut very close to the fabric, it will ravel. To prevent this, leave a 4" - 6" chain at the end of each seam. When serging across seams, rather than trimming off the extra chain, fold it to the underside of the fabric, trying not to cut it. After the seam is pulled flat, dab the thread with seam sealant, let dry, and trim the extra threads.

5. TEST - TEST - TEST. The information given is to act as a guide. Fabric and thread combinations will behave very differently.

Troubleshooting a Flatlock Stitch

Symptom: The looper thread is not reaching the cut or folded edge. ▶
- T-N-T (thread-needle-tension) - see page 61
- Loosen the looper thread tension
- Tighten lower looper tension (3-thread)
- Tighten needle thread (2-thread)
- Eliminate more fabric under the loops by decreasing the cutting width

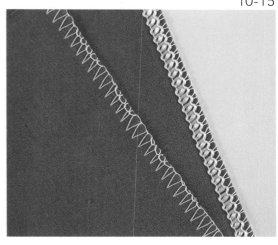

10-15

Symptom: The needle thread does not form a V-shape on the back. ▶
- T-N-T
- Loosen the needle tension
- Tighten lower looper tension

10-16

Symptom: The looper thread is loose and does not lay flat. ▶
- T-N-T
- Tighten the looper thread
- Adjust the cutting width to add fabric under the stitch

10-17

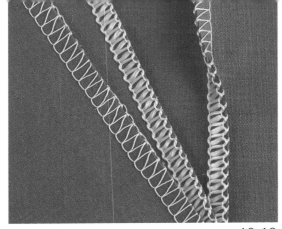

10-18

▲ **Symptom: The flatlock stitch will not form at all.**

• T-N-T

• The needle is not up as high as it will go

• Looper tensions are too loose

• Incorrectly threaded looper/needle combination

• Improper setting on automatic tension machines

10-19

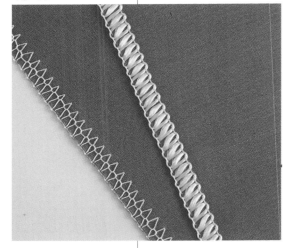

◄ **Symptom: The stitch will not flatten.**

• Loosen needle tension

• Decrease cutting width or guide the fabric
edge farther to the left

• Change to another flatlock stitch

If It Looks Like a Flatlock, Is it Always a Flatlock?

A flatlock stitch serged on a fold can be done on any fabric without worrying about
the fabric raveling. However, when the flatlock is used as the main construction
stitch on woven fabrics where the edges are not finished and will ravel, different
treatment may be required. The following techniques will add stability and strength
when flatlocking is done on a woven fabric.

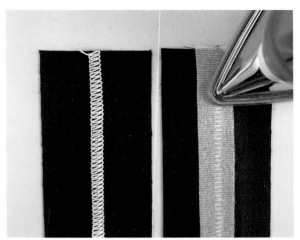
10-20

Method 1 - Fusible Interfacing #1 ▶

1. Serge a regular flatlock with the fabric wrong sides together.

2. Pull the stitch flat and lightly press open.

3. Gently press strips of fusible interfacing over the stitches on the back side of the fabric. Tricot knit interfacing will retain a soft look.

Method 2 - Fusible Interfacing #2 ▶

For small, straight areas, tricot interfacing can be fused to the edges before serging.

10-21

10-22

Method 3 - Serged Edges ▶

1. This method is best done when a wide-loop flatlock stitch is desired. Serge-finish the edges of the fabric with a narrow overlock stitch or a rolled hemstitch.

2. Serge with flatlock settings, being careful not to nick the finished edges. Guide the fabric so the loops fall off the edge. Set the

10-23

10-24

cutting width high, so the blade is as far away from the needle as possible. If the knife is raised, it's not available to cut the threads at the end of the seam or prevent the fabric from venturing too far to the right of the needle and interfering with the upper looper.

3. Gently pull the seam open and press.

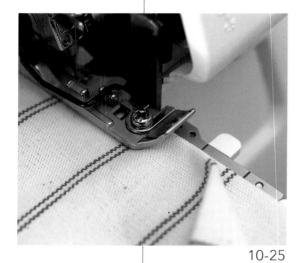

10-25

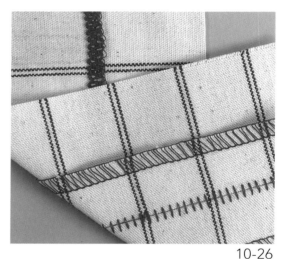

10-26

▲ **Method 4 - Fold and Serge**

1. Press the seam allowances to the wrong side. Serge finish the edge of the fabric. This step can be done first but sometimes the texture of the serged edge will press through the fabric.

2. With flatlock settings, serge the fabric together.

3. Gently pull the seam open and flat; lightly press.

False Flatlock Stitches

The following methods are known as imitation or false flatlock stitches. The finished seam looks like a flatlock, but there is more here than meets the eye. The imitation flatlock techniques can be used on loosely woven fabrics, on bulky fabrics that will not flatten, or when a strong stable seam is necessary.

Method 1- Serge and Stitch ▶

1. Serge the seam with a balanced overlock stitch.

2. Press the overlock stitch to one side.

3. Using the sewing machine, topstitch the fabric edge in place. Use monofilament or matching thread to disguise the sewing machine stitch.

Note: "Serge and Stitch" can be done in an even easier manner by using fusible thread in the lower looper. Serge, then press the seam to one side. The seam may not need to be topstitched in place since the fusible thread will adhere to the fabric. But for added security, topstitch along each edge of the stitch.

OPTIONAL: For very loosely woven or slippery fabrics, or to create a very strong seam, stitch the seam on the sewing machine first. Then serge, guiding the fabric so the needle thread stitches on the same line as the sewing machine stitching line. Press the seam to one side and topstitch in place with the sewing machine.

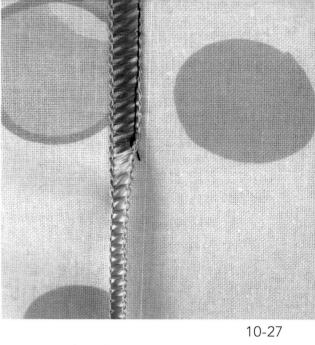

10-27

Method 2 - Stitch and Serge ▶

1. Stitch the seam on the sewing machine.

2. Using flatlock settings, serge, guiding the sewing machine stitch so it is about 1/3 of the way between the needle and the cut edge. Test and adjust the guiding as necessary.

3. Gently pull the flatlock stitch open so the sewing machine seam is covered by the flatlock stitch.

10-28

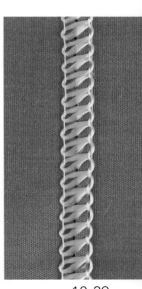

10-29

Using the Flatlock Stitch

Flatlocking is functional or decorative, strong or delicate, subtle or flashy. Commercial pattern directions will rarely suggest some of the following uses. Note how flatlocking is used in ready-to-wear and it will quickly find its way into your serger designs. It definitely is the kind of technique that the more you use it, the more you'll use it. Test all options, the 2-thread flatlock, the 3-thread flatlock, and imitation ones, to find the technique that works best.

Flatlocking can be used for most seams where a regular overlock stitch would be used. Suggestions for flatlocking fabrics that ravel have been given above. Remember that the flatlock stitch is an exposed stitch and the loops or ladders may catch or pull in some designs. Designs with many seams or patchwork are fabulous with the flatlock stitch, but extra care may be needed to secure the thread chains at the end of seams and at intersections. As a reminder, flatlocking can change the size of a garment, as much as 3/8" at each seam allowance.

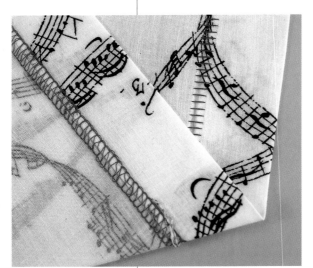

10-30

Hems

Using flatlocking to hem is a time-saver because the fabric is finished, cut off, if necessary, and hemmed in one operation. This hem finish also retains the stretch desired in knit garments.

◄ Either the loop or ladder side is appropriate on the right side. For the ladder side to show, the fabric is folded and positioned under the serger foot in the same way it is when using the blindhem stitch on the sewing machine. With flatlock settings, serge so the needle just pierces the fold. Gently pull the stitch open and press.

For the loop side to show, it is best when the right and the wrong side of the fabric are the same, or a pleasant contrast can be featured. Fold the hem up toward the right side of the garment. Then fold the hem back (like a blindhem) aligning the fold and the cut edge. Serge so the needle penetrates all three layers. Gently pull apart and press.

Flatlocking Elastic

Elastic may be flatlocked at the waistline or cuffs of ▶ lingerie or sportswear or in the middle of a piece of fabric to create a waistline or a design detail. Use a longer-than-normal stitch length to save wear and tear on the elastic. Use Woolly Nylon™ thread for a soft comfortable finish next to the skin.

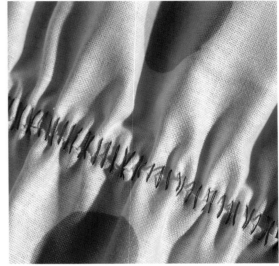

10-31

Flatlocking Fake Fur or Heavily Textured Fabric

Flatlocking simulates the same technique furriers use to ▶ assemble pelts. The edges are butted together and are truly flat. Thread the serger with monofilament or a well-matching thread. Serge with right sides together so the ladder part of the stitch is visible. After pulling the seam flat, use a wide point turner, small brush, or toothbrush to fluff the pile over the stitches.

10-32

Flatlock Fringe

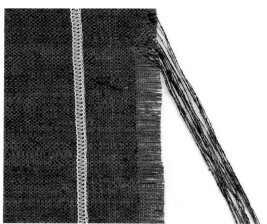

10-33

10-34

▲ The flatlock is not the fringe, but the securing stitch between the fabric and the fringe. This technique provides an interesting hemline or edge finish on scarves, place mats, or napkins. Before starting, select a fabric that will fringe easily; otherwise, it may take years to pull the threads! Determine the desired length of the finished fringe. Fold up that amount, wrong sides together, and serge with the fabric not to be fringed on the top. Use a decorative thread in the visible looper. Pull the stitch open, press lightly, and remove the threads up to the flatlock to create the fringe.

Flatlock Thread Casings

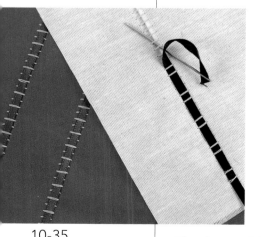

◄ The flatlock stitch can provide a perfect casing for decorative or practical purposes. For a simple but effective touch, the ladder side casing provides a grid for weaving narrow ribbon or yarn.

10-35

The loop side can be threaded with narrow, flat, or round elastic, or gimp cord for a shirring effect, for design, reinforcement, or stabilization. Row after row of elastic shirring creates a smocked effect.

Flatlocking with Lace

A narrow, 2-thread flatlock stitch is an excellent way to join fine laces or laces to fabric. Use monofilament or a fine embroidery or bobbin-weight thread and the stitch will not interfere with the beauty of the lace. A metallic thread may add interest to the flatlock stitch.

Before serging, spray-starch delicate fabrics and laces to give them additional body. Place the laces, right sides together, and guide so the needle falls in the heading of the laces. When serging lace to fabric, position the lace 1/4" from

▼ 10-36

10-37

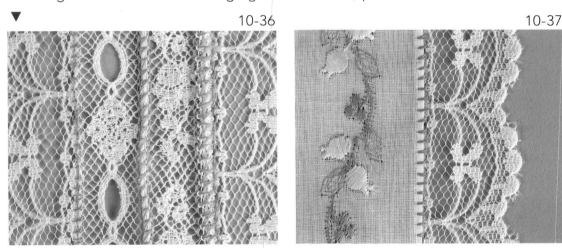

the edge of the fabric. Serge, cutting the fabric, but not the lace. Very gently pull the seam open. Remember, when doing this type of serging, you are creating the fabric first, then cutting or adapting it to the pattern.

10-38

A Final Word on Flatlocking

TEST

Creating the perfect flatlock will probably take more ▶ than one test run. Have plenty of thread and fabric handy. You may or may not need it, but it's best to be prepared. The time and energy spent testing are worth the satisfaction of the end product.

Oh No! My Serger is Sick!

When serging and getting less than perfect results, the question, "What is wrong with my serger?" is asked. Frequently, there is nothing wrong with the overlock machine; it is doing what someone told it to do! In some cases it's the machine's personality (or attitude) and often, the operator must yield and adapt. But, if a case of serger-itis does break out, there are some treatments and remedies to pursue. Your machine will be cured in a very short time. If not, take your "baby" to a serger doctor (an authorized, trained mechanic); it's probably not a serious illness and won't last long.

1. The first rule of curing serger illnesses is:
   When All Else Fails, Read the Directions.
   No further comment needed!
2. The second rule is:
   If the serger is making any strange noises, STOP SERGING.
   Continued machine operation may cause serious damage. It may just be that the machine is on a wobbly table and the table is making the noise or it could be that a thread is caught some where and continued serging will break a needle or looper. Check the serger carefully before starting to serge again.
3. Rule 3: Whatever the problem, check the obvious first!
   Is the machine plugged in?
   Is the separate light switch on?
   Is the thread pole extended as high as it will go?
   Are the correct needle plate and presser foot being used?
   Is the stitch finger correctly set?
   Is the presser foot down?
   Are the looper cover and the side door closed?
   Is the needle the proper type and size and inserted correctly?
   Have you run out of thread?
4. No obvious cure: Then check **T-N-T**
   T - THREADING
   N - NEEDLES
   T - TENSION

For a complete explanation of **T-N-T** review Chapter 4, pages 60-61, but by thoroughly and carefully checking the THREADING, NEEDLES, AND TENSION, you will solve 85% - 95% of your serger illnesses.

The following is a list of symptoms of serger illnesses and either why they occur, or a probable remedy. The remedy will depend on the fabric or thread, and stitch formation being used. Carefully try each one. If there does not seem to be a solution, walk away from the machine for a minimum of two hours, then try again. If again, things don't improve, pick up the phone and make a serger doctor appointment. Remember it's probably nothing serious, just inconvenient.

Symptom	Reason (•) or Remedy (*)
Thread breaks	* use good quality thread * change the needle(s) • thread is caught, knotted or tangled on spools, loopers, etc. • decorative thread is too weak to use • burr on upper or lower looper or needle plate • defective needle
Needle thread breaks	* use good quality thread • lower looper is threaded incorrectly • defective needle • needle is not inserted correctly
Needle breaks	* pulling of fabric while serging - let the machine do the work • tensions are too tight • defective needle • used to much speed on heavy fabrics
Skipped stitches	* insert needle correctly * loosen needle tension • defective or incorrect type or size of needle • needle tension is too tight • incorrect threading • heavy finish on fabric • uneven unwinding of thread from cone or spool • fabric is pulled while serging • burr on lower looper

Symptom	Reason (•) or Remedy (*)
Fabric jams, uneven feeding	* lower presser foot * lengthen stitch length * hold thread tail at beginning of seam * adjust presser foot pressure • trimmings are caught behind looper cover door • knives are not correctly positioned • knives are dull • thread tail is caught when forming the stitch • fabric is too bulky to serge • thread is caught, tangled, or knotted • something is blocking the feed dogs
Trimmed edge is ragged	* trim at least 1/4" of fabric when serging * starch fabric to give it more body • knives are dull • knives are out of alignment
Fabric puckers	* loosen the needle tension * serge more slowly * shorten stitch length • thread is caught, tangled, or knotted • poor thread quality • adjust differential feed to -1 • knives are dull
Fabric stretches	* set the differential feed +1 * shorten stitch length * tape seam * serge more slowly * decrease the pressure on presser foot
Noisy machine	* clean and oil machine * change the needle(s) * be sure cover and plate are screwed on tight * be sure it is the machine and not a shaky table making the noise

The Care and Feeding of Your Overlock Machine

The proper care and feeding of your overlock machine will help guarantee a long and happy serging life. Develop a routine to remind yourself to give your wonderful overlock machine a careful cleaning.

■ The frequency of the cleaning will depend on what you are serging and the machine should be cleaned inside and out. First, open the looper cover and side door. Inspect the inside and, with the brush in your accessory bag or a small soft paintbrush, remove the lint around the loopers. Be sure to brush between the knife blades and the blade and machine. Use canned air if desired, but be sure you are blowing the lint out of the machine, not up into the motor housing (See Chapter 5, Tension Disk Cleaning and Maintenance). Resist the temptation to take a deep breath and blow the lint away. The additional moisture in your breath is not welcome.

■ Next concentrate on the tension disks. See Chapter 5 for the proper cleaning methods.

■ Check your instruction manual as some machines do not have to be oiled. If yours does, the suggested oiling frequency says to oil after every eight to 10 hours of motor-running serging. If the sound of the machine changes, to a more metal-to-metal sound, you have waited too long! Oil it immediately. Be sure to use the oil provided with your machine. Oil has different consistencies and weights and using the wrong one can cause serious damage. A machine that has not been used for an extended period of time will also need to be oiled, because sewing machine oil evaporates or pools or collects when the machine sits. There are also internal parts that should be checked by a licensed mechanic.

■ Knives are very long lived and most often must be changed when they hit pins or after hours and hours of use. Directions for changing and an extra blade come with your serger, but why not use this time by taking the machine for an annual checkup?

■ The signal to change the needle is the punching sound made when a dull needle is forced through the fabric. Develop a routine to change the needles BEFORE the sound changes. Be sure to use the correct style, type, and size of needle. Next, clean the exterior of the machine, giving it a good dusting with a soft damp cloth. If you use any commercial cleaning products, use them sparingly. Spray on a cloth and wipe clean, rather than spraying the machine.

■ Finally, remember that if you take good care of your overlock machine, it will take good care of you.

A

Accessories, 22, 23, 25-27
    storage, 16, 20, 22
Accessory box, 16
Acrylic thread, 39
All-purpose thread, 35, 73, 81, 110, 128
"American thread," 31
Automatic tension, 77, 144

B

Basting, 46, 85, 93, 116
Basting tape, 93
Belt loops, 46, 133
Bias-cut fabrics, 85
Blending threads, 41
Blind hem, 116, 119, 148
Bobbins, sewing machine, 40
Bodkins, 27
Bow-making, 132
Braid, 139
Braided elastic, 116, 117
Button loops, 46, 133

C

Canned air, 76
Casings, thread, 150
Chain decorative, 133
Chainstitch, 45-46, 48-49
Chain serging, 111
Children's needle, 27
Circle, serging in a, 104
Cleaning tools, 25
Collars, rolled hem, 133
Coneholders, thread, 15, 32
Cone, thread, 30, 32, 35-39
Construction, pattern, 111, 113
Controls, 78-87
Cord, elastic, 115
Cording, rolled hem, 132
Corners, serging, 99-103
    knife window, 101
    serge-off and turn, 100
    wrapped corner or edge, 102
    inside corners, 102
Cotton thread, 35, 37, 72, 110, 124
Cover hem stitch, 49, 115
Covers, front, 15, 16, 20
Cover stitch, 49, 115, 118, 135
Cross-wound spool, 30, 31, 32, 35
"Cruise control," 19
Cupping seam, 75
Curves, serging, 103
Cutting width adjustment, 57, 74, 79, 82-83,
    124, 126, 131, 141, 143, 144, 146
Cutting width dial, 15, 16

D

Decorative thread, 21, 24, 26, 35-39, 46, 49,
    63, 73, 75, 81, 105, 121, 125, 128, 136,
        138, 140, 141, 142, 150
Decorative stitches, 44, 136
Definition, serger, 14
Differential feed, 17, 57, 79, 83-86, 110-111,
    114-116, 126-127, 130, 133, 154
Double needle, sewing machine, 116
Double-sided tape, 26

Dust removal, disk, 76-77

E

Easing fabric, 84-85, 111, 114
Edge finish, 102, 120, 127-128, 132-133, 145-151
Edge-finishing stitch, 44-48, 99, 122-133
Edge-finishing thread, 35-39, 128
Elastic, 27, 116-118
    clear, 115
    cord, 115, 118
    direct application, 118
    flatlocking, 149
    seam tape, 113
    thread, 73, 118, 150
    with casing, 118
Embroidery thread, 33, 37, 121, 151
Extension plate, 49

F

Fabric
    basting glue, 93
    decorated with
        embellishment, 87
        embroidery, 86, 87
        glitter, 86
        paint, 86
    easing, 84-85
    finish, 128, 130, 132
    guiding, 91-93
    securers, 26
    stretching, 84-85
    types
        bastiste, 73, 124, 140
        bias-cut, 85
        bulky, 21, 47, 81
        calico, 73
        chiffon, 81, 128
        cotton, 83
        cotton interlock, 108
        denim, 73
        double-knit, 108
        drapery, 73
        fake fur, 73, 140, 149
        fine, 87, 105
        fleece, 44, 73, 108, 141
        heavyweight, 19, 21, 24, 44, 81, 83, 86,
            90, 108, 117
        jersey, 108
        knits, 14, 22, 44, 45, 81, 83, 85, 86, 95,
            106-121, 133, 145, 148,
        lightweight, 19, 44, 45, 46, 73, 81, 83,
            86, 116, 121, 133, 141
        lingerie-type, 44, 121, 140, 149
        lycra, 44, 108, 113, 119-120
        medium-weight, 73, 108, 116
        napped, 86, 87
        organza, 128, 132
        slippery, 86, 93, 121, 147
        taffeta, 81, 132
        tapestry, 73
        terry, 108
        tricot, 121, 145
        tulle, 128
        velour, 73, 83, 108,
        woven, 22, 85, 105, 133, 144-146, 147

weight, 73
Feed dogs, 20, 21, 22, 58, 80, 83, 84, 86-87, 92, 110, 114-115
Finger, screw, presser foot, 87
"Finish and turn" hem, 116
Fishing line, 132
Flat bed insert, 49
Flatlocking, 37, 38, 39, 118, 134-151
    cutting width, 141
    fabric, 140
    fusible interfacing, 145
    imitation or false flatlock, 146-147, 148
    needles, 140
    stitch, types of, 45, 46, 121, 134-151
        2-thread, 137, 138, 139, 143, 148, 151
        3-thread, 137-139, 143, 148
        4-thread, 139
        safety stitch, 139
    thread, 140
    serged edges, 145, 146
    stitch length, 141
    stitch width, 141
    troubleshooting, 143-144
    uses
        casings, 150
        elastic, 149
        fake fur, 149
        fringe, 150
        hems, 148
        lace, 151
        textured fabric, 149
    woven fabrics, 144-146
Floss threader, Butler dental, 52, 55
Flossing disks, 77
Foot control
    connection, 17
    socket, 19
    "cruise control" setting, 19
Fray Check™, 94
Free arm, 16, 17
Fringe, 46, 150
Front cover, 15, 16, 20
Fusible interfacing, 145
Fusible thread, 39, 105, 116, 147
Fusible web, 105

G

Gathering, 85
Glue sticks, 26, 93
Grain, fabric, 131
Guiding the fabric, 91-93, 141-142, 144, 145, 147, 151

H-J

Handwheel, 15, 16, 17, 18
"Hare" symbol, 19
Hemming, 105, 115, 116, 148
Hemostats, 27, 52
Holding layers of fabric, 92-93
Home decorating items, 48
Inside corners, serging, 102
Imitation or false flatlock, 146
Jet-Air™ threading system, 53

K

Knife, 21, 59, 90, 114

Adjustment of, 15, 49, 53, 57, 146
Care, 22, 155
Dull, 22
Lower, 82
Moving side to side, 22
Upper, 49, 82
Window, 101, 104
Knit picker, 95
Knits, 14, 22, 44, 45, 81, 83, 85, 86, 95, 133, 145, 148, 106-121
Knitted elastic, 116

L

Lace, 140, 141, 151
Ladders, 136
LED screen, 16, 52, 77
Lettuce-edge finish, 120, 133
Light switch, 18
Lingerie elastic, 118
Lint removal, disk, 76-77
Looper, 20, 54, 69, 74, 92, 124, 127, 129, 140
    cover, 20, 53, 91
    lower, 54, 55, 57, 69, 70, 116, 126-127, 128, 138, 139, 147
    ribbons, 38
    stitches, 44-49
    tension, 75, 127, 130-131, 143-144
    thread, 20, 35-39, 41, 44, 68, 69, 70, 71, 73, 74, 81, 97, 99, 110, 116, 126-127, 128-129, 133, 136-139
    threading, 55, 57, 62
    upper, 54, 57, 58, 69, 70, 126-127, 128, 131, 138, 139, 146
Loop turner, 95
Loops, 136

M

Machine, serger, See Serger machine
Maintenance
    machine, 25, 155
    tension disks, 76-77
Matching threads, 41
Metallic thread, 24, 25, 37, 38, 124, 151
Mode, serger, 9
Monofilament thread, 36, 140, 147, 149, 151

N

Needle plate, 15, 16, 17, 21, 22, 63, 91, 124
Needle, 23-25, 45, 91
    double-eye, 95
    eye, 23, 25, 30, 97
    household, 23
    identifying code numbers, 23
    industrial, 23
    inserting, 23, 24
    left, 24, 41, 54, 68, 69, 74, 82, 90, 124, 130
    right, 69, 74, 82, 24, 54, 69, 82, 90, 124
    sizes, 25, 27, 109, 120
    stitches, 44-49
    stop, 17
    tension, 69, 74, 126, 130, 137, 139
    thread, 20, 35, 36, 37, 44, 68, 69, 70, 74, 96-99, 110, 127, 133, 137, 138, 140, 143
    threading, 56, 63, 144
    threaders, 27, 56
    T-N-T, 60-61, 71, 143-144, 152-153

troubleshooting, 25, 61, 63, 74-75, 92, 133

types
  ballpoint, 24, 109
  children's, 27, 95
  embroidery, 24, 124
  flatlocking, for, 140
  quilting, 25
  rolled hem, for, 124
  sharp, 24
  specialized, 24, 27, 109
  tapestry, 27, 95
  topstitch/jeans, 24
  universal, 109, 120, 121, 124
No-Fray™, 94
Nylon thread, 36, 73, 110, 127, 128, 138, 149

O

Overlock, See also Stitch, types
  definition, 14
  stitch, 20, 45-47, 66, 67, 68-71, 79, 96, 145, 147
Outside corners, serging, 100

P-Q

Packaging thread, 30-34
Paper clips, 26
Parallel-wound spool, 30, 31, 32
Parts, identifying serger, 15-22
Pattern, matching, 85
Pearl cotton thread, 115, 132
Pinning, 92-93, 114
Pins, super-sized, 26
Plaid, matching, 85
Pneumatic threading system, 53
"Pokies," 131
Polyester thread, 35, 39, 72, 120, 121, 128
Polymer thread, 37, 39
Power connection, 17
Power switch, 17, 18, 19
Presser foot, 15, 16, 17, 20, 22, 53, 56, 57, 58, 62, 79, 86-87, 90, 92, 96, 103, 112, 121, 124, 141, 142
  adjustment, 86-87
  lifter, 20, 59, 90
  options, 20, 49
  pressure, 79
Puckers, preventing, 121, 126, 130, 154

R

Rayon thread, 37, 72, 124, 128
Ready-to-wear, 14, 48, 49, 139, 148
Removing seams, 97-99
Resources, 160
Rethreading, 18, 30, 32, 50-63
Reversible stitch, 136
Ribbing, 85, 113-115
Ribbon, 38, 115, 150
Ribbon floss, 38
Rippling, fabric, 86
Rolled hem, 82, 86, 96, 100, 120, 122-133
  adjustment, 124
  collars, 133
  fabric selection, 127
  needle, 124
  problems/solutions, 129-132

setup, 126-127
stitch, 46, 121, 124-133, 145
stitch length, 125
stitch width, 124
tension settings, 126
thread selection, 127-128
uses, 132-133
Ruffles, making, 85

S

Seams, 91-104
  guiding the fabric, 91-93
  hemming, 105
  removing, 97-99
  securing, 94-97
Serging corners, 99-103
Serging curves, 103
Serging in a circle, 104
Serging speed, 19, 31, 32, 59, 142, 154
  slide switch, 19
  symbols, 19
Seam line, 91
Seam ripper, surgical, 99
Seam sealant, 94, 104, 142
Seam taping, 112
Securing the seam, 94-97
"Select 'N' Sew" stitch selection, 17
"Serge and Stitch," 147
Serger machine, 12-27
  definition, 14
  hems, 105
  maintenance, 25, 155
  mode, 9
  needles, 23-25
  noise, 155
  parts, identifying, 15-22
  seams, 91-104
  tools, 25-27
  troubleshooting, 152-154
Setup, machine, 52-57, 109-111, 126-127
Sewing machine comparison, 10-11, 18, 21, 31, 40, 44, 45, 47, 58, 68, 82, 86, 89, 91, 99, 102, 103, 105, 110-111, 116, 148
Side cover, 15, 16, 20, 53, 80
Silk ribbon, 38
Skeins, thread, 38, 39
Smocked, 150
Spool base and pins, 19, 32, 40
Spool cap, 31, 32
Spools
  parallel-wound, 30, 31
  cross-wound tube, 30-31, 32
  cones, 30, 31, 32, 35-39, 71
Spray starch, 128, 130, 132, 151
Stabilizer, wash away, 132
Stitch
  finger, 22, 82, 96-97, 101, 104, 124, 125
  length, 80-81, 125, 131
  length adjustment, 15, 17, 57, 68, 74, 79, 83, 125, 131, 141
  selection, 17, 44
  stretching fabric, 84-86
    controlling stretch, 112, 154
    testing for stretch, 108-109

testing, 58
T-N-T, 60-61, 71, 143-144, 152-153
troubleshooting, 60-61, 92
types
    2-thread chainstitch, 45-46, 77
    2-thread overlock, 45, 48, 77, 126, 128
    3-thread overlock, 20, 46, 47, 48, 77,
        97, 102, 105, 110, 114, 118, 120,
        121, 124, 126, 128, 130, 139
    4-thread overlock, 20, 44, 47, 48, 54,
        68, 69, 74, 77, 82, 97, 100, 102,
        105, 110, 114, 118, 120, 124, 139
    5-thread, 48
    basting, 46
    blind hem, 116, 119, 148
    chainstitch, 45-46, 48-49
    cover hem stitch, 49
    cover stitch, 49
    flatlock, See Flatlocking
    overedge, 46
    rolled hem, 46, 121, 124-133, 145
    safety stitch, 47, 48, 69
width, 22, 68, 74-75, 82-83
    rolled hem, 124
    flatlocking, 141
Switches
    light, 18
    power, 18
    slide, 17, 19, 22, 67, 87, 96
    speed setting, 19

T

Tape, seam
    types, 112, 113, 115, 132
Tape, thread, 26
Taping guide, 112, 115
Tassels, 46, 133
Techniques, mastering, 88-105
Tension, 64-77
    adjustment, 52, 53, 57, 61, 62, 64-77, 81,
        83, 135-139, 141
        rolled hem, 129-132
    definition, 66
    dials, 15, 16, 54, 66, 67
    disks, 30, 53, 54, 56, 60, 62, 72, 130
        maintenance, 76-77
    knobs, 66, 67
    needle, 69, 74, 126, 130, 137, 139
    problems, 25, 30, 36, 53, 69, 70, 71, 127
    reference system, 67, 68
    slides, 66, 67
    slots, 16, 17, 54, 56, 130
    T-N-T, 60-61, 71, 143-144, 152-153
Thickness, fabric, 73
Thread, 28-41
    adapter, 16
    buying, 40
    casings, 150
    chain, 59, 90, 94-96, 121, 133, 142, 148
    coneholders, 15, 32
    cutter, 59
    looper, See Loopers
    guide pole, 15, 16, 17, 19, 52
    guides, 20, 30, 52-57, 60, 62, 71

labeling codes, 33
matching, 40, 41
multiple strands, 24
packaging, 30-34
quality, 30, 33
needle, See Needle
raveling, preventing, 142
selection of, 34-39
stand, 15, 19, 31, 32
tail, 95, 97, 99, 100, 101, 104
tapes, 26
T-N-T, 60-61, 71, 143-144, 152-153
types, 34-39, 72
    all-purpose, 35, 73, 81, 110, 128, 129
    blends, 35, 38, 39
    cotton thread, 33, 35, 37, 72, 110, 124
    decorative, See Decorative threads
    embroidery, 33, 37, 121, 151
    metallic thread, 24, 25, 37, 38, 124, 151
    monofilament thread, 36, 140, 147,
        149, 151
    novelty, 24, 73, 75, 81, 124
    pearl cotton, 115, 132
    polyester thread, 35, 39, 72, 120, 121,
        128
    polymer thread, 37, 39
    variegated, 129
    topstitching, 33, 46, 105, 116, 119, 147
    Woolly Nylon™, 36, 120, 121, 125, 128,
        129, 130
    tubes, 35, 37, 38, 39
    weight, 33
Thread breaking, 18
Threaders, 27, 52, 55, 56
Threading, 50-63, 27, 53, 140
    diagram, 20
    elastic, 27
    problems, 18, 30, 72
    sequence, 53, 57, 60, 71
    shortcuts, 62-63
"Three-foot rule," 77
Tools, 23, 25-27, 52
"Tortoise" symbol, 19
Trash receptacle, 17
Trims, decorative, 46
Troubleshooting, 152-154
    stitch, 60-61
    tension, 61, 76-77
    looper, 127
Tweezers, 22, 27, 52, 55, 56
"Tying-on" threads, 62

U-Z

Waving, fabric, 85, 86
Weight, fabric, 73
Weight, thread, 33
Wire, floral, 132
Woolly Nylon™ thread, 36, 120, 121, 125, 128,
    129, 130
Wool yarn, 39
Woven elastic, non-roll, 117
Wrapped corner or edge, 102
Yarn, 39, 73, 140, 150